OCR SHP GCSE

BRITAIN IN PEACE AND WAR

1900–1918

CHRISTOPHER
CULPIN

HODDER
EDUCATION
AN HACHETTE UK COMPANY

The Schools History Project

Set up in 1972 to bring new life to history for school students, the Schools History Project has been based at Leeds Trinity University since 1978. SHP continues to play an innovatory role in history education based on its six principles:

- Making history meaningful for young people
- Engaging in historical enquiry
- Developing broad and deep knowledge
- Studying the historic environment
- Promoting diversity and inclusion
- Supporting rigorous end enjoyable learning

These principles are embedded in the resources which SHP produces in partnership with Hodder Education to support history at Key Stage 3, GCSE (SHP OCR B) and A level. The Schools History Project contributes to national debate about school history. It strives to challenge, support and inspire teachers through its published resources, conferences and website: http:// www.schoolshistoryprojectorg.uk

This resource is endorsed by OCR for usc with specification OCR Level 1/2 GCSE (9–1) in History B (Schools History Project) (J411). In order to gain OCR endorsement, this resource has undergone an independent quality check. Any references to assessment and/or assessment preparation are the publisher's interpretation of the specification requirements and are not endorsed by OCR. OCR recommends that a range of teaching and learning resources are used in preparing learners for assessment. OCR has not paid for the production of this resource, nor does OCR receive any royalties from its sale. For more information about the endorsement process, please visit the OCR website, www.ocr.org.uk.

The publishers thank OCR for permission to use specimen exam questions on pages 102–105 from OCR's GCSE (9–1) History B (Schools History Project) © OCR 2017. OCR has neither seen nor commented upon any model answers or exam guidance related to these questions.

Note: The wording and sentence structure of some written sources have been adapted and simplified to make them accessible to all pupils while faithfully preserving the sense of the original

Although every effort has been made to ensure that website addresses are correct at time of going to press, Hodder Education cannot be held responsible for the content of any website mentioned in this book. It is sometimes possible to find a relocated web page by typing in the address of the home page for a website in the URL window of your browser.

Hachette UK's policy is to use papers that are natural, renewable and recyclable products and made from wood grown in sustainable forests. The logging and manufacturing processes are expected to conform to the environmental regulations of the country of origin.

Orders: please contact Bookpoint Ltd, 130 Park Drive, Abingdon, Oxon OX14 4SE. Telephone: (44) 01235 827720. Fax: (44) 01235 400454. Email education@bookpoint.co.uk Lines are open from 9 a.m. to 5 p.m., Monday to Saturday, with a 24-hour message answering service. You can also order through our website: www.hoddereducation.co.uk

ISBN: 978 1 4718 6107 9

© Chris Culpin 2016

First published in 2016 by
Hodder Education,
An Hachette UK Company
Carmelite House
50 Victoria Embankment
London EC4Y 0DZ

www.hoddereducation.co.uk

Impression number   10 9 8 7 6 5 4 3 2 1

Year   2020 2019 2018 2017 2016

Cover photo: ©IWM

Typeset by White-Thomson Publishing Ltd

Printed in Italy

A catalogue record for this title is available from the British Library.

CONTENTS

Introduction

Making the most of this book

 Where this book fits into your GCSE history course

The course

The GCSE history course you are following is made up of five different studies. These are shown in the table below. For each type of study you will follow **one** option. We have highlighted the option that this particular book helps you with.

OCR SHP GCSE B

(Choose one option from each section)

Paper 1 1 ¾ hours	**British thematic study** ● The People's Health ● Crime and Punishment ● Migrants to Britain	**20%**
	British depth study ● The Norman Conquest ● The Elizabethans ● Britain in Peace and War	**20%**
Paper 2 1 hour	**History around us** ● Any site that meets the given criteria.	**20%**
Paper 3 1 ¾ hours	**World period study** ● Viking Expansion ● The Mughal Empire ● The Making of America	**20%**
	World depth study ● The First Crusade ● The Aztecs and the Spanish Conquest ● Living under Nazi Rule	**20%**

The British depth study

The British depth study focuses on a short time span when the nation was under severe pressure and faced the possibility or actual experience of invasion. The point of this study is to understand the complexity of society and the interplay of different forces within it. You will also learn how and why historians and others have interpreted the same events and developments in different ways.

As the table shows, you will be examined on your knowledge and understanding of the British depth study as part of Paper 1. You can find out more about that on pages 98 to 105 at the back of the book.

Here is exactly what the specification shows for this depth study.

Britain in Peace and War, 1900–1918

The specification divides this depth study into five sections:

Sections and issues	Learners should study the following content:
Wealth *Issue: Tensions in Edwardian society*	• Britain's power and wealth at the beginning of the twentieth century: an overview of industry, empire, military strength, technology and cities • Class distinctions: the lives of the upper, middle and working classes • Rowntree's investigation into the nature of poverty
Politics *Issue: Threats to political stability*	• Strengths and weaknesses of the established parties and the rise of the Labour Party • The Liberal reforms, the People's Budget, the clash with the Lords and the Parliament Act of 1911 • The challenge from militant labour including the crisis years between 1910 and 1914
Women *Issue: The nature and extent of support for women's suffrage*	• Women's lives at the beginning of the twentieth century • The campaigns for the vote: suffragists, suffragettes, support and opposition • The relationship between Government responses and changes to the campaigns, 1910–1914
Empire *Issue: British attitudes towards the Empire*	• Differing attitudes towards the British Empire at the beginning of the twentieth century including responses to the Boer War • India: differing British attitudes towards the Raj, 1900–1914 • Ireland: differing attitudes to the Home Rule crisis, 1912–1914
War *Issue: Responses to the demands of total war*	• Government policy and propaganda in response to the changing demands of war including early recruitment, conscription and DORA • Men's responses to the demands of the war including volunteering, pals' battalions and conscientious objection • Women's responses to the demands of the war including volunteering, employment and developments in the suffragette campaign

You need to understand the interplay between these forces in society:
● Political
● Economic
● Social
● Cultural.

You need to pay special attention to this underlying issue:

How and why the period 1900–1914 has been interpreted as a 'golden age' and the reasons why this interpretation has been challenged.

You should study a range of types of interpretation including:
● academic (historians)
● educational
● popular (e.g. television)
● fictional.

The next two pages show how this book works.

How this book works

The rest of this book (from pages 8 to 97) is carefully arranged to match what the specification requires. It does this through the following features:

Enquiries

The book is largely taken up with five 'enquiries'. Each enquiry sets you a challenge in the form of an overarching question.

The first two pages of the enquiry set up the challenge and give you a clear sense of what you will need to do to work out your answer to the main question. You will find the instructions set out in 'The Enquiry' box, on a blue background, as in this example.

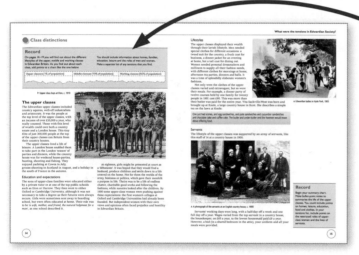

Record tasks

From that point, the enquiry is divided into three sections. These match the bullet points shown in the specification on page 3. You can tell when you are starting a new section as it will start with a large coloured heading like the one shown here. Throughout each section there are 'Record' tasks, where you will be asked to record ideas and information that will help you make up your mind about the overarching enquiry question later on. You can see an example of these 'Record' instructions here. They will always be in blue text with blue lines above and below them.

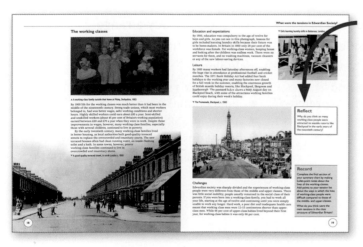

Reflect tasks

At regular intervals we will set a 'Reflect' task to prompt you to think carefully about what you are reading. They will look like the example shown here.

These Reflect tasks help you to check that what you are reading is making sense and to see how it connects with what you have already learned. You do not need to write down the ideas that you think of when you 'reflect', but the ideas you get may help you when you reach the next Record instruction.

Review tasks

Each enquiry ends by asking you to review what you have been learning and use it to answer the overarching question in some way. Sometimes you simply answer that one question. Sometimes you will need to do two or three tasks that each tackle some aspect of the main question. The important point is that you should be able to use the ideas and evidence you have been building up through the enquiry to support your answer.

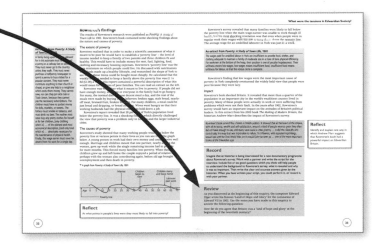

Closer looks

Between the enquiries you will find pages that provide a 'closer look' at some aspect of the theme or period you are studying. These will often give you a chance to find out more about the issue you have just been studying in the previous enquiry, although they may sometimes look ahead to the next enquiry.

We may not include any tasks within these 'closer looks' but, as you read them, keep thinking of what they add to your knowledge and understanding. We think they add some intriguing insights.

One very important final point

We have chosen enquiry questions that should help you get to the really important issues at the heart of each period you study, but you need to remember that the examiners will almost certainly ask you different questions when you take your GCSE. Don't simply rely on the notes you made to answer the enquiry question we gave you. We give you advice on how to tackle the examination and the different sorts of question you will face on pages 98 to 105.

A Golden Age?

This is a photograph of Henley Regatta in 1912. These rowing races, still held on the River Thames each year, are properly called Henley Royal Regatta, because members of the royal family usually attend. In this photo the fine barge being rowed on the far side of the river, was built in 1689 and under the canopy at the rear are King George V and Queen Mary. The rowers in the crowd salute the king and queen by holding up their oars. The regatta is an opportunity for people to dress up and enjoy a summer picnic on a boat on the river. The photograph seems to show a serene, traditional, idyll – a Britain enjoying a 'Golden Age'.

▲ Henley Regatta in 1912

▲ Holidaymakers in deckchairs at Blackpool, Lancashire

This photograph from about the same time is of crowds enjoying the sunshine by the sea at Blackpool, Lancashire. Some of the men are wearing the straw hats called 'boaters', but others are wearing the working man's flat cap. There are well-dressed women and girls wearing the larger, decorated hats of the period. It is not as fashionable a scene as Henley, but nonetheless relaxed and happy, perhaps another picture of a British 'Golden Age'.

But Britain in 1912 was far from being relaxed and serene. Women had re-started their campaign for the vote with new anger, smashing shop windows and burning houses. There were massive strikes in many industries, sometimes violent. One newspaper warned that the country was in 'a dangerous state' and some gunshops in London ran out of weapons. Parliament had only just emerged from a long drawn out conflict, with two General Elections in 1910. And in Ireland hostile groups were getting hold of arms and training for what looked like a looming civil war.

For some, at least, this was hardly a 'Golden Age'.

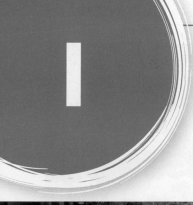

'Land of Hope and Glory'?

What were the tensions in Edwardian Society?

▲ The official painting of Edward VII's coronation in 1902, by Edwin Abbey

On 22 January 1901, Queen Victoria died and her 64-year reign came to an end. The crown passed to her son, who became King Edward VII. His short reign, from 1901 to 1910, is known as the Edwardian period.

Edward VII's coronation in Westminster Abbey on 9 August 1902 was a splendid ceremony. The painter Edwin Abbey was chosen as the official artist of the coronation. In his painting above, you can see King Edward as he is about to be crowned, surrounded by church leaders and members of the aristocracy dressed in their ceremonial robes.

New pieces of music were specially written for the coronation. King Edward suggested that Britain's most famous composer, Edward Elgar, should add words to one of his tunes. The result was 'Land of Hope and Glory'. Elgar's song celebrated Britain's power in the world and the freedoms enjoyed by her people.

Reflect

What impression of the coronation ceremony do you think the artist Edwin Abbey wanted to give?

Tensions

The summer of 1902 was a tense time for the organisers of the coronation. The 59-year-old king was fond of large meals and cigars. He was overweight and often unwell. The coronation had originally been planned for 26 June, but, three days before, Edward developed appendicitis and required immediate surgery. The operation took place on a table in the music room at Buckingham Palace. The next day, Edward was sitting up in bed smoking cigars, but the coronation had to be postponed.

For months, towns and villages across Britain had been planning their coronation celebrations. Now they had to decide what to do. The villagers of Croxley Green near London decided to go ahead. They had decorated their village with bunting and had planned a procession, maypole dancing and a re-enactment of a Boer War battle. The children were looking forward to the tea party and to the Punch and Judy show. However, the celebrations of Croxley Green were not free from trouble.

In the nearby town of Watford, some people were not happy that the celebrations there had been postponed. A mob of angry young men gathered in the streets and began to cause trouble. The villagers of Croxley Green were afraid that the mob would come to their village. At the local police station, 40 local volunteers were sworn in as special constables. They made the cricket pavilion their headquarters and patrolled the roads on bicycles to keep a look out. In the end, although the Watford 'roughs' never appeared in Croxley Green, the villagers' celebrations had been disturbed by an unseen threat. In June 1902, the 'land of hope and glory' was also a country of social divisions where the possibility of disturbance, and even violence, was never far from the surface.

▼ A tea ticket from the Croxley Green coronation celebrations

The Enquiry

The pomp and splendour of Edward VII's coronation could not hide some underlying tensions in Britain at the beginning of the twentieth century. In the Edwardian period, Britain was the wealthiest and most powerful country in the world, but it faced some serious challenges. As you will discover, many people in Britain were desperately poor and the lives of women were particularly restricted. In addition, Britain's place as the leading world power began to be challenged by other countries.

In this enquiry you will learn about:

- Britain's power and wealth at the beginning of the twentieth century
- Class distinctions in Edwardian Britain
- The shocking findings of one man's investigation into the lives of poor people.

At the end of the enquiry you will decide how far you agree with the idea that Edwardian Britain was a 'land of hope and glory'.

Industry

As you know, in the period 1750–1850, Britain was the first nation in the world to experience an Industrial Revolution. By 1900, industry and trade had made Britain the world's richest country. Four main industries accounted for half of Britain's industrial output and employed a quarter of the workforce: textiles, iron and steel, coalmining and shipbuilding.

During the nineteenth century, Britain had developed an efficient transport system to support her industrial expansion. By 1900, the rail network covered 20,000 miles and no village was more than 20 miles from a railway station. British steamships carried people and goods across the world.

The workers

In Edwardian Britain, industries created a wide range of jobs for working people. Skilled manual workers could earn good wages. Britain's industries also provided millions of jobs for semi-skilled and unskilled workers. Edwardian men found regular work as miners, quarrymen, builders, factory workers and warehouse-men. The work of unskilled labourers, however, was often hard and unpleasant, and their wages were low. Anyone without a job faced poverty and hardship as there was no unemployment benefit in 1900.

For Edwardian women, the opportunity to earn a wage was more limited. In the north of England women were employed in the textile mills of Lancashire and Yorkshire. In other parts

▲ Industrial workers in Lancashire, c. 1900

of Britain, women worked in factories, laundries and shops. However, the only option for many working-class girls was to work as a domestic servant in the houses of the upper and middle classes.

Threats from abroad

By 1900 Britain was facing competition from other countries. In the last part of the nineteenth century, the gap in industrial production between Britain and her nearest rivals, Germany and the USA, had narrowed. Edwardians were worried by these threats to British industrial supremacy. They realised that there were disadvantages to being the first country to industrialise. British iron- and steel-works, factories, shipyards and mines often used out-dated equipment and had no room to expand. Many British industrialists had not invested their big profits in new, larger plants.

Empire

More than anything else, it was the Empire which made Edwardian Britain such a wealthy and powerful country. The red shaded areas on the map (right) show the extent of the British Empire in 1902. By then, Britain ruled a quarter of the land on the globe and a fifth of the world's population. The lines across the ocean show the under-sea cable telegraph which linked what were seen as the most important parts of the Empire.

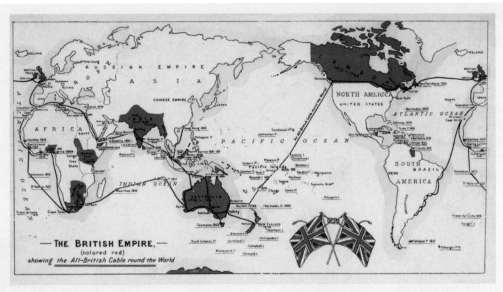

▲ A map of the British Empire, 1902

Opportunities

In 1900 the Empire offered many opportunities for British business. The British Empire produced a wide range of raw materials and provided a huge market for the products of manufacturing industry in Britain. Investors put money into imperial businesses such as railways, mines and plantations producing sugar, tea, coffee and rubber. The British Empire also offered opportunities to Edwardians who wanted to make a new life in the colonies. In the early 1900s millions of migrants from Britain boosted the populations of Canada, Australia and New Zealand.

▼ British officials in India, sitting in rickshaws pulled by their Indian servants, c. 1900

Tensions

Behind the glorious British Empire represented in Elgar's 'Land of Hope and Glory' there were tensions. The song suggested that the Empire should expand 'wider still and wider', but this did not happen. During Edward VII's reign, hardly any new territories were added to the British Empire. In fact, the Empire became the focus of criticism. The Boer War, which Britain had fought in South Africa between 1899 and 1902, cost much money and many lives. Many people in Britain began to turn against the war as it dragged on.

At the beginning of the twentieth century, some people began to question whether the Empire was a source of wealth, or a drain on it. They argued that the money invested in the Empire would be better spent on modernising British industry. In addition, some people in Britain and in the colonies were beginning to criticise the Empire for its exploitation of colonised people and for its use of brute force to protect British interests.

Record

Make a spider diagram for 'Empire'. Include examples of how the Empire made Britain powerful and wealthy. Use a different colour to add any tensions.

Military strength

By the early twentieth century, Britain's enormous wealth had enabled it to become a major military power. As an island, dependent on foreign trade and possessing a huge empire, Britain's military might lay in her navy. On the eve of the First World War in 1914, the Royal Navy had 68 battleships, 121 cruisers and 64 submarines. Some of them can be seen in this photograph of the review of the fleet at Spithead near Portsmouth in 1914.

▲ The Naval Review at Spithead, near Portsmouth, 1914

In 1906 the British launched a new type of battleship, the *Dreadnought*. This ship was so technically advanced that it made existing battleships obsolete. It had thicker armour, ten 12-inch guns which could sink an enemy battleship ten miles away and a crew of 800. The steam turbine engines (another British invention) gave the *Dreadnought* a speed of 22 knots. Germany soon began building its own version of the *Dreadnought* and a hugely expensive arms race began. By 1914 Britain had built 29 of these formidable battleships, Germany 17.

But what if the next war was not going to be fought at sea? The tiny British Army in 1914 consisted of just a quarter of a million regular soldiers, with half a million reservists. The Kaiser could call on 8 million soldiers in the German army.

Technology

Advances in technology accelerated after 1900 and these began to transform people's lives in Britain:

▼ A motor car, c. 1910

- Motor cars began to appear on British roads although they were far too expensive for all except the rich.
- In 1901 the Italian inventor Marconi used enormous kites to lift radio aerials high into the sky and sent a wireless signal from America to England.
- Moving pictures were first shown in 1896 and immediately became popular. After 1900, cinemas began to be built in towns across Britain.
- Electricity provided a new source of power. At home, electric lights were replacing gas and the streets took on a new look as electric trams replaced horses.
- Typewriters and telephones were changing how businesses operated
- Portable electric vacuum cleaners were changing housework.

Not all these advances in technology were developed in Britain. The typewriter, the telephone and the home vacuum cleaner were invented in the USA, while the best motor cars and the fastest steamships were being produced by Germany.

Record

Make two more spider diagrams for 'Military strength' and 'Technology'.

◀ The city of London, c. 1900. The main buildings are the Bank of England on the left, and the Royal Exchange, on the right

Cities

By 1900, there were 50 cities in Britain with a population of over 100,000. With 77 per cent of the population living in towns and cities, Britain was the most urbanised country in the world. By far the largest city was London, with a population of 7 million.

In 1900, London and other great urban centres such as Birmingham, Leeds, Manchester, Newcastle and Glasgow were horse-drawn cities, with buses, carts and private vehicles all pulled by horses. The smell of horse manure was everywhere and street-sweepers were employed to make sure you could cross the street without getting your shoes dirty. By 1918 the scene was quite different, as motorised buses, cars and electric trams had taken over.

The centres of Britain's cities were full of magnificent buildings: town halls, department stores, baths, libraries, concert halls, theatres, glittering pubs, music halls, and the newest craze – cinemas. By 1900 many of the horrors of early industrial cities – the over-crowding, bad sanitation and killer-diseases – had been overcome. However, close to the city centres you could still find areas of slum housing where the poor lived in overcrowded and insanitary conditions.

▼ A photograph of slum housing in London, c. 1900. One family's possessions are on the street because they have been evicted.

Reflect

What can the photograph tell us about the wealth and power of London at the beginning of the twentieth century?

Record

Make your final spider diagram for 'Cities'. Remember to use a different colour when adding any tensions or problems you have found.

Think carefully about the information you have recorded on your five spider diagrams. From what you have discovered so far, what do you think were the biggest tensions in Edwardian Britain?

Class distinctions

Record

On pages 14–19 you will find out about the different lifestyles of the upper, middle and working classes in Edwardian Britain. As you find out about each class, add points to a chart like the one below.

You should include information about homes, families, education, leisure and the roles of men and women. Make a separate list of any tensions that you find.

Upper classes (1% of population)	Middle classes (19% of population)	Working classes (80% of population)

▶ Upper-class boys at Eton, c. 1910

The upper classes

The Edwardian upper classes included country squires, well-off industralists and aristocrats. It was the people at the top level of the upper classes, with an income of over £10,000 a year, who really counted. Those with this level of wealth could own both a country estate and a London house. This tiny élite of just 300,000 people at the top of the upper classes ran Britain from their country houses.

The upper classes lived a life of leisure. A London house enabled them to take part in the London 'season' of parties and dinners, while the country house was for weekend house-parties, hunting, shooting and fishing. They enjoyed yachting at Cowes in July, grouse-shooting in Scotland in August, and a holiday in the south of France in the autumn.

Education and expectations

The sons of upper-class families were educated either by a private tutor or at one of the top public schools such as Eton or Harrow. They then went to either Oxford or Cambridge University, although it was not necessary to take a degree as their futures were always secure. Girls were sometimes sent away to boarding school, but were often educated at home. Their role was to be *a wife, mother, and friend, the natural helpmeet for a man*', as one school described it.

At eighteen, girls might be presented at court as a 'débutante'. It was hoped that they would find a husband, produce children and settle down to a life centred on the home. Not for them the worlds of the army, business or politics, which gave their menfolk a purpose in life. Theirs was to be a life of endless chatter, charitable good works and following the fashions, while nannies looked after the children. By 1900 some upper-class women were pushing against these expectations: the first women's colleges at Oxford and Cambridge Universities had already been founded. But independent women with their own views and opinions often faced prejudice and hostility in Edwardian Britain.

Lifestyles

The upper classes displayed their wealth through their lavish lifestyle. Men needed special clothes for different occasions: a tweed suit for the country, a frock coat for business, a dinner jacket for an evening at home, but a tail coat for dining out. Women needed personal dressmakers and milliners to supply all their fashion needs, with different clothes for mornings at home, afternoon tea parties, dinners and balls. It was a time of splendidly elaborate women's fashions.

Not only were the clothes of the upper classes varied and extravagant, but so were their meals. For example, a dinner party of twelve courses held by one family for twenty people in 1901 cost £60. This was more than their butler was paid for the entire year. Vita Sackville-West was born and brought up at Knole, a large country house in Kent. She describes a simple tea on the lawn at Knole:

▲ Edwardian ladies in Hyde Park, 1905

> One just had scones, and egg sandwiches, and pate sandwiches and cucumber sandwiches and chocolate cake and coffee cake. The butler and under-butler and the footmen would move about offering food.

Servants

The lifestyle of the upper classes was supported by an army of servants, like this staff of 14 at a country house in 1900.

▲ A photograph of the servants at an English country house, c. 1900

Servants' working days were long, with a half-day off a week and one full day off a year. Wages varied from the top servant in a country house, the housekeeper, on £65 a year, to the lowest housemaid paid £9 a year. However, a bed (in a shared bedroom in the attic), your uniform and all your meals were provided.

Record

Begin your summary chart. Make bullet-point notes to summarise the life of the upper classes. You could include points on homes, leisure, education, food and clothes. In your tensions list, include points on the restricted roles of upper-class women and the lives of servants.

▼ A lower-middle-class family in their garden, c. 1900

The middle classes

The middle classes were an important part of Edwardian society. The growth of business, the civil service, education and local government led to an increasing number of middle-class jobs. At the upper end were higher professionals, like lawyers, doctors and senior business managers, earning up to £5000 a year. At the lower end were teachers, clerks and police sergeants, on about £100 a year. £100 was a big social dividing line, because with this income a family could just about afford one servant (a 'maid-of-all-work'), usually a teenage girl.

Education and expectations

The sons of the middle class were educated at a public school or a grammar school and were expected to start a career when they left school. Hours were long, even for managers, and people were expected to work on Saturday mornings. Middle-class girls, on the whole, led less restricted lives than their upper-class counterparts. Girls' schools were springing up for the daughters of the middle classes. While some of these had an academic curriculum, most girls' schools focused on cookery, hygiene, laundry and housewifery.

Most girls worked when they left school. Technology brought new jobs for girls, as typists, telephonists and secretaries. Few middle-class women had professional jobs, and those who did paid a big price: they had to stay single, because on marriage women were expected – even compelled in some jobs like teaching and the Civil Service – to stop work.

It is hard to generalise, but there is some evidence that the new century brought changes to marriage. The subservient wife of Victorian times was giving way, in many couples, to a more equal partnership. Nevertheless, the life of a middle-class married woman centred around children and the home. Her main task was to manage the servants – perhaps a cook, and a maid or two in a household in the middle of this middle class. Some middle-class Edwardian women were beginning to feel frustrated by their dull and restricted lives.

Servants in middle-class households had to work hard. One servant, Hannah Cullwick recorded in her diary how a typical day's work began:

> Up at 6.30 – opened the shutters and lit the kitchen fire – emptied the soot, swept and dusted the room and the hall, laid the breakfast table – cleaned 2 pairs of boots – 9 o'clock, made tea for the master and mistress – made the beds and emptied the slops* , cleared and washed up the breakfast things ….
>
> [*Slops. With no toilet in their rooms, the family used pots for their needs, which had to be carried downstairs to be emptied.]

Lifestyles

The middle classes could afford new, well-built and good-sized homes. They often lived in detached 'villas' or in large semi-detached houses in the most pleasant areas of towns. It was still the fashion for the middle classes to fill their new homes with furniture, carpets, fittings and ornaments, However, by 1900, some families were turning away from heavy, cluttered rooms towards more simple interiors. This trend continued during the Edwardian period as it became more difficult to find servants to do the cleaning and dusting.

▲ The interior of an upper-middle-class house, c. 1900

Middle-class families enjoyed a wide range of leisure activities. As the picture below shows, tennis was particularly popular, for women as well as men. Golf was popular with middle-class men, but when women took up the sport they clashed with all-male golf club committees. The middle classes went cycling, visited theatres and cinemas, and in the winter, took part in a new craze – board games.

▼ *The Tennis Party*, a painting by Charles March Gere, 1905

Record

Complete the middle section of your summary chart by making bullet-point notes about the lives of the middle classes. Remember to list any further tensions which you have discovered.

The working classes

▲ A working-class family outside their home at Pilsley, Derbyshire, 1903

By 1900 life for the working classes was much better than it had been in the middle of the nineteenth century. Strong trade unions, which most workers belonged to, had won better wages, safer working conditions and shorter hours. Highly skilled workers could earn about £80 a year. Semi-skilled and unskilled workers (about 45 per cent of Britain's working population) earned between £60 and £70 a year when they were in work. Despite these improvements in wages, however, many working-class families, especially those with several children, continued to live in poverty.

By the early twentieth century, many working-class families lived in better housing, as local authorities built good-quality terraced streets to replace the overcrowded and insanitary courts. The new terraced houses often had clean running water, an inside flushing toilet and a bath. In some towns, however, poorer working-class families continued to live in overcrowded and insanitary slums.

▼ A good-quality terraced street, in north London c. 1900

Education and expectations

By 1900, education was compulsory to the age of twelve for boys and girls. As you can see in this photograph, lessons for girls included learning laundry skills because their future was to be home-makers. In Britain in 1900 only 29 per cent of the workforce was female. For working-class women, keeping house and looking after the children was endless work. There were no servants for them, and no washing machines, vacuum cleaners or any of the new labour-saving devices.

Leisure

By 1900 many workers had Saturday afternoons off, enabling the huge rise in attendance at professional football and cricket matches. The 1871 Bank Holiday Act had added four bank holidays to the working year and many factories now closed for a full week in the summer, enabling the enormous growth of British seaside holiday resorts, like Blackpool, Skegness and Scarborough. The postcard below shows a busy August day on Blackpool beach, with some of the attractions working families could enjoy during their week's holiday.

▼ Girls learning laundry skills in Battersea, London, c. 1907

▼ The Promenade, Blackpool, c. 1900

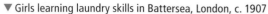

Reflect

Why do you think so many working-class people were attracted to seaside resorts like Blackpool in the early years of the twentieth century?

Challenges

Edwardian society was sharply divided and the experiences of working-class people were very different from those of the middle and upper classes. There was little social mobility; people usually remained in the social class of their parents. If you were born into a working-class family, you had to work all your life, starting at the age of twelve and continuing until you were simply unable to work any longer. Hard work, a poor diet and inadequate health care meant that working class men were 12–15 centimetres shorter than upper-class men. While 96 per cent of upper-class babies lived beyond their first year, for working-class babies it was only 66 per cent.

Record

Complete the final section of your summary chart by making bullet-point notes about the lives of the working-classes. Add points to your tension list about the ways in which the lives of working-class people were difficult compared to those of the middle- and upper-classes.

What do you think were the main tensions in the class structure of Edwardian Britain?

● Rowntree's revelations

▲ Poor children in the East End of London, c. 1905. They are part of a family of nine.

Reflect

What signs of poverty can you see in this photograph?

In 1900, children like these were to be found in the back streets of Britain's towns and cities. Few middle- and upper-class people ever went into the districts where the poor lived. Important questions about the lives of Britain's poorest people therefore remained unanswered: Who were the poor and how did they live? Exactly how many people lived in poverty? Why were they poor when the country was so prosperous?

At the end of the nineteenth century some investigators had begun to find out about the London poor, but there was still much ignorance about their lives. In 1900, there were three widely held views about the poor:

- The poor were a relatively small proportion of the population.
- The poor nearly all lived in London and the big industrial cities.
- If people were poor, it was often because they were lazy or chose to spend their wages in the pub.

The Times newspaper expressed this third view in 1902:

their wages would suffice to keep them strong and healthy, but they are thriftless; they drink and bet, or they are ignorant and careless in housekeeping.

Rowntree's investigation

One man decided to carry out a proper investigation to test these assumptions. Seebohm Rowntree was the son of Joseph Rowntree, the wealthy owner of a large chocolate factory in the city of York. As you know, most boys from upper-class families went to public school and then to Cambridge or Oxford, but Seebohm Rowntree did neither. The Rowntrees were Quakers, outside the mainstream of the Church of England, so he went to a local school in York, and then to Owens College in Manchester, where he studied chemistry.

Seebohm Rowntree's Quaker background gave him a strong social conscience and he thought it was his duty to help the poor. In 1899, at the age of 28, he decided to carry out an investigation into poverty in York. Everyone knew that poverty was a problem in London and in some of the big industrial cities, but little was known about a medium-sized city like York. Parts of the city were very well off, but York had slum districts where many poor families struggled to make a living. Rowntree was determined to discover how poor people in York lived, and exactly what caused their poverty.

Seebohm Rowntree's approach was to be as scientific as possible. He made no judgements in advance, and simply started to collect evidence. Rowntree and his team of investigators studied all the working class districts of York. They visited the homes of 11,560 families, making detailed notes on the work, living conditions, incomes and expenditure of working-class people. Rowntree's survey was the most extensive and systematic study ever undertaken of the lives of the poor in an ordinary English town.

▲ Seebohm Rowntree, c. 1920

▼ Families in Hungate, York, c. 1901

Reflect

Why do you think people would be unable to ignore Rowntree's findings?

Rowntree's findings

The results of Rowntree's research were published as *Poverty: A Study of Town Life* in 1901. Rowntree's book contained some shocking findings about the nature and causes of poverty.

The extent of poverty

Rowntree realised that in order to make a scientific assessment of what it meant to be poor he would have to establish a 'poverty line' – the level of income needed to keep a family of two parents and three children fit and healthy. This would have to include money for rent, fuel, lighting, food, clothing and necessary housing expenses. Rowntree's 'poverty line' was the bare minimum on which people could live. He discussed with nutritionists what foods made up a healthy lifestyle, and researched the shops of York to see where these items could be bought most cheaply. He calculated that the weekly income needed to keep a family above the poverty line was £1 1s 8d (£1.08) a week. His report contained a powerful description of what this would mean for the lives of poor families. You can read an extract on the left.

Rowntree was very clear what it meant to live in poverty. If people did not have enough money, someone or everyone in the family had to go hungry. For many, the normal diet was one decent meal a day, and the rest of the meals were made by buying cheap leftovers: broken eggs, stale bread, nearly-off meat, bruised fruit, broken biscuits. For many children, a meal could be just bread and dripping, or bread and jam. Wives went hungry so that their working husbands had the physical energy to hold down a job.

Rowntree's report revealed that 28 per cent of York's population lived below the poverty line. It was a shocking finding which directly challenged the view that poverty was a problem only in London and the larger industrial cities.

The causes of poverty

Rowntree's study showed that many working people would dip below the poverty line at various points in their lives as you can see from the graph below. A young person in work had their own money and could survive well enough. Marriage and children meant that one partner, nearly always the woman, gave up work while the single remaining income had to provide for more mouths. This forced many families into poverty. When their children grew up and left home the couple enjoyed a period of relative ease, perhaps with the woman also contributing again, before old age brought unemployment and then death in poverty.

▼ A graph from *Poverty: A Study of Town Life,* 1901

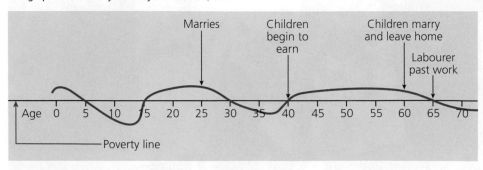

An extract from *Poverty: A Study of Town Life*, 1901

A family living upon the scale allowed for in this estimate must never spend a penny on a railway fare or omnibus. They must never go to the country unless they walk. They must never purchase a halfpenny newspaper or spend a penny to buy a ticket for a popular concert. They must never contribute anything to their church or chapel, or give any help to a neighbour which costs them money. They cannot save, nor can they join sick club or Trade Union, because they cannot pay the necessary subscriptions. The children must have no pocket money for dolls, marbles, or sweets. The fathers must smoke no tobacco, and must drink no beer. The mother must never buy any pretty clothes for herself or for her children, [only clothing which is] … of the plainest and most economical description, [and only food which is] … absolutely necessary for the maintenance of physical health. Finally, the wage earner must never be absent from his work for a single day.

Reflect

At what points in people's lives were they most likely to fall into poverty?

Rowntree's survey revealed that many families were likely to fall below the poverty line when the main wage-earner was unable to work though ill health, but his most shocking revelation was that even when people were in regular work their wages were too low to keep them above the poverty line. The average wage for an unskilled labourer in York was just £1 a week.

An extract from *Poverty: A Study of Town Life*, 1901

The wages paid for unskilled labour in York are insufficient to provide food, shelter, and clothing adequate to maintain a family of moderate size in a state of bare physical efficiency. For workmen at the bottom of the heap, their position is one of peculiar hopelessness. Their unfitness means low wages, low wages means insufficient food, insufficient food means unfitness for labour, so that the vicious circle is complete.

Rowntree's finding that low wages were the most important cause of poverty in York completely overturned the widely held view that people were poor because they were lazy.

Impact

Rowntree's book shocked Britain. It revealed that more than a quarter of the population in an important city in the world's wealthiest country lived in poverty. Many of these people were actually in work or were suffering from problems which were not their fault. In the years after 1902, Rowntree's survey would have an important impact on the attitudes of Britain's political leaders. In this extract from his 2009 book *The Making of Modern Britain*, the historian Andrew Marr describes the impact of Rowntree's survey.

Rowntree's book arrived like a bomb in British politics. It showed that at the heart of the empire, with all its pomp, wealth and self-satisfaction, around a third of people were so poor they often did not have enough to eat, and many were sunk in utter poverty … It did this clinically and statistically, in a way that was impossible to refute. Its influence, with repeated reprintings, would last until the First World War and it would later be seen as … one of the most important books of the Edwardian age.

Reflect

Identify and explain one way in which Andrew Marr suggests that Rowntree's book had a powerful impact on Edwardian Britain.

Record

Imagine that an historian is being interviewed for a new documentary programme about Rowntree's survey. Work with a partner and write the script for the interview. Include five or six good questions which you think will help people to understand the background to Rowntree's survey, what it revealed and why it was so important. Then write the clear and accurate answers given by the historian. When you have written your script, you could perform it, or record it, with your partner.

Review

As you discovered at the beginning of this enquiry, the composer Edward Elgar wrote his famous 'Land of Hope and Glory' for the coronation of Edward VII in 1902. Use the notes you have made in this enquiry to answer the following question:

How far do you agree that Britain was a 'land of hope and glory' at the beginning of the twentieth century?

▲ The Worthing Excelsior Cycling Club in 1913

The cycling craze

In the years before the First World War there was a huge craze for cycling. Victorian bicycles had been difficult to ride, uncomfortable, even dangerous. A British invention, the 'Safety Bicycle' had solved these problems. Edwardian bicycles had equal-sized wheels, good brakes, gears for tackling hills, inflatable rubber tyres and more comfortable saddles. Most importantly, the new bicycles were affordable.

In the years before the First World War, cycling clubs became extremely popular. It is hard for us to imagine the sense of freedom cycling brought. For many Edwardians, getting out into the countryside on their bicycle at the weekend brought a welcome escape from the town, office and factory. With 'Cyclists' Maps' and the company of new friends, cyclists could venture far from home.

As you will discover in Enquiry 3, many women in this period were seeking to change their lives. Buying a bicycle and joining a cycling club opened up all kinds of new freedoms for women. As you can see, the Worthing Excelsior Cycling Club was a mixed-gender club, with men and women enjoying cycling expeditions together, meeting members of the opposite sex as part of the crowd. Special 'ladies' bicycles', like those on the opposite page, were designed to allow women to cycle while wearing the long skirts which women were expected to wear.

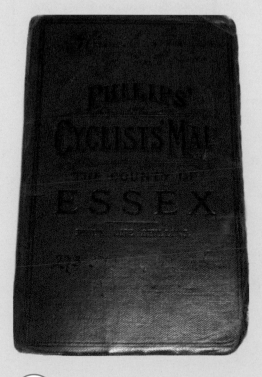

◀ A Philips' Cyclists' Map from 1900

▲ Advertisement for a lady's bicycle, c. 1910

▲ Advertisement showing a female cyclist wearing bloomers, c. 1900

Nevertheless, it must have been difficult to cycle in a long skirt and some women took to wearing 'bloomers'. These garments brought outraged criticism from more old-fashioned observers who were, it seems, scandalised by bloomer-wearing women showing at least 9 inches of their legs.

One of the most famous and successful cycling clubs was the Clarion Cycling Club, which had 8000 members in branches all over the country. Its members were socialists and took the name from *The Clarion*, a socialist newspaper edited by Robert Blatchford. They put their socialist principles into action through the 'good fellowship' they showed on their cycling jaunts. They also sold *The Clarion* wherever they went, and stuck red gummed labels with socialist slogans on trees and gateposts as they went. They also set up Clarion Clubhouses to rest and have tea, like this one at Handforth, Cheshire.

▶ A Clarion Club house at Handforth, Cheshire

Shaken to its foundations?

Was there any real threat to Britain's political stability, 1900–14?

This is Robert Gascoyne-Cecil, Lord Salisbury, three times Prime Minister of the United Kingdom (1885–6, 1886–92, 1895–1902). At the General Election of 1900 his Conservative Party won easily. His fellow government ministers were, like him, all expensively educated, wealthy and confident men.
Salisbury summed up his view of government when he said:

Whatever happens will be for the worse and therefore it is in our interest that as little should happen as possible.

▲ Engraving of Robert Cecil, Lord Salisbury, made c. 1900

◀ Hatfield House in Hertfordshire, c. 2011

This is Lord Salisbury's family home, Hatfield House, about 25 miles north of London. It had been owned by his family since his ancestor Robert Cecil built it in 1611. In the sixteenth century, Robert Cecil, like his father William, had served Queen Elizabeth I as her most trusted adviser. The Cecil family stood as a symbol of continuity and political stability in British history.

The Enquiry

With Lord Salisbury's election victory in 1900, that stability seemed set to continue. But, in one opinion, expressed recently on a website, events in the years shortly before 1914 'shook the British state to its foundations' as centuries of political tradition faced a real threat of change. According to this view, the social tensions you learned about in Enquiry 1 were acting like powerful, hidden forces that cause earthquakes as they began to shake the world of British politics.

In this enquiry you will learn about:

- The strengths and weaknesses of the established political parties and about the rise of the Labour Party
- How the Liberal Party tried to deal with problems of poverty and how this caused a major constitutional crisis
- How organised groups of working people took militant industrial action to try to improve their lives.

At the end of each section you will need to decide how great the threat was to Britain's political stability. You will show your decision on a continuum line like this:

No threat
to stability

Serious threat
to stability

Parliament and political parties in 1900

In 1900, as now, there were two Houses of Parliament: the House of Commons and the House of Lords. They each played a part in making new laws. The Lords (peers) had the right to sit in the House of Lords simply by having a title but Members of Parliament (MPs) were elected to the House of Commons by voters.

The vote

- Only about one-third of all adults had the right to vote in elections.
- Women did not have the vote (you'll find out more about this in Enquiry 3).
- Only about two-thirds of men had the vote, at age 21. A male voter had to be head of a household or a lodger who had lived at the same address for at least a year.
- The vote also went with owning property worth a certain amount (what this sum had to be varied from place to place) ...
- ... or being a university graduate.

(These last two meant that some men had more than one vote.)

The House of Commons

Members of Parliament (MPs) who were elected to serve in the House of Commons were not paid, so only those with a private income could afford to become an MP.

The House of Lords

As we noted on page 14, rich landowners dominated British society. Many, like Lord Salisbury, were also peers. The House of Lords was made up mainly of hereditary peers with some Church of England bishops. Peers had a role in government as members of the House of Lords but many of their relations were also members of the House of Commons. Ten of the nineteen members of the Conservative Cabinet of 1900 were members of the House of Lords, including Lord Salisbury, the last Prime Minister to sit in the House of Lords. This gave the House of Lords a much more equal role in government with the House of Commons than it has today.

When a new law is being discussed it is a 'Bill'; when it has been passed by both Houses it becomes an 'Act'. The Lords could criticise and even change bills put before them by the government, although it was normally accepted that they would not change bills dealing with finance, like the budget.

▲ The Houses of Parliament at Westminster, London, c. 1900

The established political parties in 1900

The political situation in 1900 had not changed much in the previous 50 years. It seemed a very stable system. The same two parties, the Conservative Party and the Liberal Party, usually alternated in power.

The Conservatives

- Supported by landowners and the majority of middle-class voters.
- There was also considerable working-class support, with many Conservative Working Men's Clubs. This drew on a feeling of deference and respect for those above them. *'Those in a position of education were the authority and the people to govern. They knew best'* as an Oxford bricklayer's labourer put it.
- The Conservatives were the party of support for the Church of England, the British Empire and agriculture.
- In general the Conservatives opposed change.
- Conservatives had a permanent majority in the powerful House of Lords, outnumbering Liberal peers by seven to one. This, of course, remained the same whichever party won an election for the House of Commons.
- The Conservatives won 335 seats in the 1900 election.

Their leader was Lord Salisbury until he retired in 1902 when his nephew Arthur Balfour took over as leader and also became Prime Minister.

▲ Arthur Balfour, c. 1900

The Liberals

- Supported by those members of the working class who had the vote and a substantial minority of the middle class.
- Supported by the popular Non-Conformist Christian churches such as the Methodists, Baptists, Congregationalists, etc.
- Supported particularly by active trade unionists. Trade-union financial support enabled a few working men to become MPs. They were mainly miners, and sat with the Liberals as 'Lib-Labs'.
- The Liberals were the party of gradual reform. They believed in encouraging individual liberty, thrift and self-reliance.
- The Liberals won just 183 seats in the 1900 election.

Their leader was Herbert Asquith. From a middle-class Yorkshire mill-owning family, he went to Oxford University and became a successful lawyer. He served as Prime Minister between 1908 and 1916.

▲ Herbert Asquith, c. 1900

Irish Nationalist Party

- The whole of Ireland was part of the United Kingdom and was represented in Parliament with 106 seats.
- The biggest Irish party was the Irish Nationalists, which won 82 of the seats in the 1900 election.
- Campaigned for Irish Home Rule by peaceful means.
- On other issues usually supported the Liberals.

The leader of the Irish Nationalists was John Redmond. He was born in the family mansion on their estate in County Wexford.

▲ John Redmond, c. 1900

Reflect

How would you sum up the strengths and weaknesses of the two main parties?

How do you think each would deal with the social problems in Britain which Rowntree had revealed (see Enquiry 1)?

The rise of the Labour Party

The stability of the old two-party system was to be disrupted by the rise of a new party, the Labour Party. By 1924, Labour had replaced the Liberals as the main opposition party to the Conservatives and a new two-party system was firmly established for the rest of the twentieth century.

Two quite different groups came together in the late nineteenth century to form the Labour Party:

- **Socialists**

  In 1848 Karl Marx fled from Germany to London. In his books – *The Communist Manifesto* and *Das Kapital,* he argued that under the economic system called capitalism, privately owned businesses – factories or farms, banks or shops – exploit the many workers by using their labour for the benefit of the rich few. He called for a revolution to overthrow this system.

  Some middle-class intellectuals took up Marx's ideas to throw out the ruling classes in a socialist revolution. Others rejected the idea of revolution and set up the Fabian Society to campaign for gradual socialism.

- **Trade unions**

  A few trade unionists joined middle-class socialist societies, but most trade unions had no interest in socialism, or even in politics. They were committed to improving the position of their members by negotiation with employers, including, as a last resort, strikes.

The leadership of Keir Hardie

The key figure in bringing these two strands together was Keir Hardie. He argued that the interests of employers, who were all either Conservatives or Liberals, were bound to be in conflict with the interests of workers; he was not satisfied with a few working men sitting with the Liberals as 'Lib-Labs'. He was elected to Parliament in 1892 and helped to set up the Independent Labour Party (ILP) in 1894.

Hardie's speeches and his appearance in the clothes of a Scottish miner outraged the House of Commons. In June 1894 he was shouted down for criticising the House for sending a message of congratulation to the Duke and Duchess of York on the birth of their son while ignoring a mining disaster in Wales on the same day in which 250 miners were killed:

> Everyone will rejoice in a quiet way with the Duke and Duchess of York on the birth of their child, but it is to the sore-stricken poor of that Welsh valley that the true hearts of this great nation will turn with overwhelming sympathy. The life of one Welsh miner is of greater commercial and moral value to the British nation than the whole Royal crowd put together, from the Royal great grandmama down to this puling Royal great grandchild.
>
> Two hundred and fifty human beings, full of strong life in the morning, reduced to charred and blackened heaps of clay in the evening. Woe, woe unutterable everywhere throughout that Welsh valley … We are a nation of hypocrites.

But he and all the other ILP candidates were defeated at the next election and the party struggled, with no money and little support.

◀ A sketch of Keir Hardie, c. 1903

Political action

In the 1890s, the Conservative government restricted the activities of trade unions. A conference of socialist societies, the ILP and some trade unions met in 1900 and formed the Labour Representation Committee, soon called the Labour Party. Links between unions and formal political activity were growing.

These links grew stronger later that year as a result of a strike by railway workers on the Taff Vale Railway. After the strike was settled, the Railway Company sued the union for loss of income and was awarded £42,000. This legal decision was disastrous for all unions – it made strike action impossible as they would soon lose all their funds. Unions realised that they needed a change in the law, which meant supporting the Liberals and the Labour Party. Only 30 per cent of unions had supported the setting up of the Labour Party back in 1900; by 1906 nearly 60 per cent did so. In 1903, the Liberals also made an agreement with Labour not to stand against each other in elections where they thought a single opposition candidate could beat the Conservatives. This 'Lib-Lab pact' as well as support from the unions helped to give the Labour Party 29 MPs in the 1906 election.

Reflect

What were the strengths and weaknesses of the Labour Party by 1906?

Political fears and suspicion

Although the new Labour MPs were prepared to work with the Liberals, the relationship was an uneasy one. Hardie made clear his position on working with the Liberals in 1892:

> If the Liberals are prepared to accept our principles, we are prepared to work with them. If they are not, they are no more our friends than the Tories.

The Liberals too were uneasy about the rise of an alternative party seeking working class votes. In 1909, the cartoonist Bernard Partridge published this cartoon that summed up how many Liberals felt about their ties to the socialism of the Labour Party from 1903 onwards.

Reflect

Political cartoons are not really meant to make us laugh out loud, although they may bring a smile to our face by putting across one view of a complicated situation in a simple drawing.

1. Which two parties are represented here?
2. How does the cartoonist see the relationship between them?
3. What impression does he give of socialism?
4. The caption tells you what the man on the left is saying and thinking. How do these show what the cartoonist thinks is the future of the two parties? (Note: he was right!)

Record

Make the first of your 'continuum lines' under the heading 'Parliament and political parties in 1900' (see page 27). Tick the circle that you think best shows the level of threat to political stability by 1906. Underneath this, explain your decision by using evidence from pages 28–31.

▲ A political cartoon from 1909 called 'Forced Fellowship'. The man on the left is saying: 'Any objection to my company, guv'nor? I'm a-goin' your way …' (and quietly to himself, he adds) '… and further'

The Liberal reforms

The Liberals won a landslide victory in the 1906 election, taking 397 seats to the Conservatives' 156. There were three main reasons for their overwhelming victory:

1. The Conservatives had led the country into the Boer War but this did not end in the expected glorious British victory. The war had cost £22 million and nearly 6000 British soldiers had been killed. Liberal opposition to the war, which had got them into a lot of trouble in 1900, now seemed justified and there were doubts about the whole idea of the Empire (See Enquiry 4).
2. Lib-Lab pact (see page 31).
3. The 'big loaf and the little loaf': The Conservatives supported a policy of 'Imperial Preference'. That is, food and other goods coming into Britain from the countries of the Empire could do so freely, but those coming in from elsewhere in the world would have to pay an import tariff. The Liberals made much of this, saying it would put up the price of food. Liberal election posters compared the 'little loaf' of 'Imperial Preference' with the 'big loaf' of free trade.

▼ David Lloyd George and Winston Churchill, 1910

'New Liberalism'

The old nineteenth-century Liberal Party believed in what was called *laissez-faire*; that is, government's only role was to free individuals to look after themselves, to 'stand on their own two feet'. They followed the common view that if people were in poverty it was their own fault. The government would help those in such distress that they were in danger of dying by providing workhouses set up under the Poor Law. But life in a workhouse was deliberately made very harsh, in order to discourage people from relying on them.

Leading figures in the new Liberal government, were fiery new ministers David Lloyd George, the Chancellor of the Exchequer, (left) and Winston Churchill, who was also a minister (right). They were clear that, for far too many people, this non-intervention was not working. The 'New Liberals' wanted to abandon *laissez-faire*. As Rowntree and other researchers had convincingly shown, too many people, through no fault of their own, were unable to 'stand on their own two feet'. Only the government could step in to help people at those points in their lives when they were vulnerable or in difficulties. As Winston Churchill put it in a speech in Dundee 1908:

> We want to draw a line below which we will not allow a person to live and labour, yet above which they may compete with all the strength of their manhood.

New Liberalism meant a dramatic change in the role of government, playing a part in people's lives which it had never done before. There were several reasons for this:

- **Rowntree's shocking report on poverty in York** (see page 22). With 28 per cent of the city's population unable to lead decent, healthy lives and many more experiencing dire poverty at some time in their lives, the current system was obviously not working.

- **The rise of the Labour Party** was a threat to the Liberals, who now had to show that they could deal effectively with working-class concerns. In 1906 they quickly passed the Trades Disputes Act. This reversed the Taff Vale judgement (see page 31) and was an attempt to win support from trade unions.

- **Socialism.** There was widespread fear of socialism and anxiety that people whose lives were desperate enough would support the violent revolution which some socialists called for.

- **Rivalry with Germany.** The German government had introduced old age pensions and schemes to help workers when they were unable to work through illness or injury. British visitors to Germany admired these welfare measures and argued that a fit, secure workforce was essential for an industrialised nation.

- **The poor health of army recruits.** Poverty was a threat to the nation. How could the armed forces find enough men to defend the country if half the males were not fit to carry arms?

> ## Reflect
>
> Which of these reasons do you think was most likely to make the Liberals want to do more to provide for people's needs?

Priority groups

The two groups who were least able to 'stand on their own two feet' were children and old people.

Children

The Liberals passed a number of laws to help children.

Councils were allowed to provide school meals from 1906, although this was not compulsory until 1914. By then, 9 million school meals a day were being provided. Good health in childhood is essential to a healthy adult life, so school medical checks were introduced in 1907.

The 'Children's Charter' tried to help children who were in trouble with the law. Up until then no distinction was made between child and adult law-breakers so many children ended up in adult prisons. The Liberals set up borstals for young offenders instead, as well as juvenile courts.

Old people

Old age pensions were introduced in 1908. Individuals over the age of 70 received 5s (25p) a week. Married couples received 7s 6d (37½p). The pension was paid to any person who had lived in Britain for twenty years, provided they were not a drunk and had an income of less than 12s (60p) a week. When some Conservatives argued against pensions, the Labour MP Will Crooks (the first MP to have been born in a workhouse), replied to one objection:

> Who are you to be continually finding fault? … if a man is foolish enough to get old, and has not been artful enough to get rich, you have no right to punish him for it. They are veterans of industry, people of almost endless toil.

◀ A grandmother and grandchild, from a family photograph, c. 1900

Sickness and unemployment

The greatest cause of poverty identified by Rowntree was loss of income through sickness or unemployment: Lloyd George set about tackling this problem. Many workers paid for insurance against sickness and unemployment through Friendly Societies or their trade union. However, lower paid workers could not afford the insurance subscriptions: about half the working population had no insurance at all. Lloyd George's plan, based on the model used in Germany, was for the government to run a national insurance scheme. The scheme had two parts:

National Insurance, Part I – sickness
Every worker earning under £160 a year had 4d (1.7p) a week deducted from their wages. To this, the employer had to add 3d (1.25p) and the government 2d (0.8p). Workers thus got 9d (3.75p) worth of insurance. In return, a worker could claim 10s (50p) a week sickness pay for up to 26 weeks, and then 5s (25p), plus free medical care.

National Insurance, Part 2 – unemployment
This covered seven industries, such as building, where occasional unemployment was a common problem. Again, it was an insurance scheme. Workers, employers and the government paid 2½d (1p) a week each. Unemployment benefit of 7s (35p) a week was paid for up to 15 weeks and the payments were made at the new Labour Exchanges, opened in 1910.

In each case the basic Liberal values of encouraging self-reliance can be seen: the amount of benefit paid was not enough to live on and workers had to pay something themselves. The time limits in the unemployment scheme meant that individuals could not be idle but had to find work as soon as they could. The intention was to attract working-class support without putting off the middle classes.

The Liberals made the most of this appeal with posters like this. It shows Lloyd George sitting at the bedside of a sick worker, as if he is a doctor caring for his patient. He points out the benefits of his National Insurance scheme.

Reflect

What can this poster tell us about the aims of the Liberal government?

THE DAWN OF HOPE.

NATIONAL INSURANCE AGAINST SICKNESS AND DISABLEMENT

Mr. LLOYD GEORGE'S National Health Insurance Bill provides for the insurance of the Worker in case of Sickness.

Support the Liberal Government
in their policy of
SOCIAL REFORM.

▶ A poster issued by the Liberal government, 1911. It aims to show how Lloyd George's National Insurance will be a comfort to sick workers

The People's Budget, 1909

Every one of these social reforms had to be paid for by the government. This could not be done without raising taxes. This job would have to be tackled by David Lloyd George, the Chancellor of the Exchequer in Asquith's Liberal government.

In 1908 this cartoon appeared, showing Lloyd George as a highwayman. He and his horse are waiting at a crossroads. He has a gun and is all set to commit a robbery, forcing people to part with their valuables against their will.

▼ David Lloyd George as a highwayman. A cartoon from the magazine *Punch*, 1908

Reflect

The cartoonist calls Lloyd George 'The philanthropic [generous and kind] highwayman'.

1. Whom do you think Lloyd George is about to rob?
2. How does the cartoonist suggest that Lloyd George will use the money he has taken for the good of others?

Increasing taxes

The Liberals' social reforms were not the only government priority that would need large sums of money. Lloyd George also had to find money to build more battleships to keep pace with German naval expansion (see page 12), so he needed to find an additional £16 million.

When he presented his 'People's Budget' in April 1909 he proposed several increases in taxation:

- Income tax was raised from 1/- (5p) in the pound to 1/2 (6p) on unearned income e.g. money from rents, and incomes over £3000.
- A further 6d (2½p) was levied on incomes over £5000.
- There were taxes on petrol and motor cars.
- But the most controversial was the tax of 20 per cent on the unearned profits from selling land.

PUNCH, OR THE LONDON CHARIVARI.—August 5, 1908.

THE PHILANTHROPIC HIGHWAYMAN.

Mr. Lloyd-George. *"I'LL MAKE 'EM PITY THE AGED POOR!"*

Without this budget the Liberals' social reforms simply could not happen. The budget's passage through Parliament created a crisis that seriously challenged Britain's constitution (the rules about how the country was ruled). This 'Constitutional Crisis' lasted two years and was an important landmark in how Britain is governed.

The Constitutional Crisis 1909–11

April 1909

Lloyd George presents the People's Budget.

The members of the House of Lords had a large permanent Conservative majority. Most were concerned to protect landowners like themselves whose wealth would be hit by the People's Budget. It caused outrage among the Lords. Some went so far as to call it a 'socialist revolution'.

November 1909

The People's Budget is overwhelmingly thrown out by House of Lords.

Against all normal Parliamentary practice, the House of Lords rejected the budget. Lloyd George was furious. He accused them of making a revolution likely by rejecting his budget. He threatened to sweep the House of Lords away. Here is what he said about the House of Lords and its landowners in October 1909:

> Should 500 men, ordinary men chosen accidentally from among the unemployed, override the judgement of millions of people who are engaged in the industry which makes the wealth of this country? That is one question. Another will be: who ordained that a few should own the land of Britain? Who made us trespassers on the land of our birth?

January 1910

General Election: Liberals stay in power.

The Liberals called a General Election to demonstrate democratic support for their budget. They won but only just. They no longer had an overall majority and were now dependent for votes on support from Labour and Irish Nationalist MPs.

Reflect

This is a Liberal Party poster. How do you think it attempted to win the support of voters?

▶ A Liberal poster from the January 1910 General Election. On the left it shows the voters (all men). On the right are the Lords or peers

April 1910 House of Lords passes the budget.	The Liberals were now determined never to let the peers overrule the Commons again and planned to weaken the House of Lords permanently.
May 1910 Negotiations begin on how to limit the power of the House of Lords.	These negotiations between the Conservatives and the Liberals took a long time, partly because King Edward VII died in May. Parliament was occupied with arrangements for the funeral and then the coronation of the new king, George V.
November 1910 Negotiations break down.	After the collapse of negotiations, the Liberals called another General Election to gain a democratic mandate to reform the House of Lords.
December 1910 **General Election**	The Liberals campaigned on the slogan 'The peers v. the people'. The result showed little change to the position of the parties and the Liberal government continued.
July 1911 House of Commons passes the Parliament Bill.	**The Commons proposed three really important changes:** 1. House of Lords cannot reject a finance bill. 2. House of Lords can only hold up a bill passed by the House of Commons for a maximum of two years. 3. MPs were to be paid, so that ordinary people without a private income could enter Parliament.
August 1911 House of Lords narrowly decides to reform itself.	Before it could become law, the Parliament Bill had to pass the Lords. They were furious at how it would reduce their traditional powers, but their position was weak after two Liberal election victories. The Liberals threatened to get the king to create 500 new Liberal peers to out-vote the Conservative majority. Faced with this threat, the Lords gave way and agreed to pass the Parliament Act.

Reflect

At which date do you think the constitutional crisis was at its most serious?

Record

Under the heading 'The Liberal Reforms' make your second 'continuum line' (see page 27). Tick the circle that you think best shows how great was the threat to political stability between 1906 and 1911. Underneath this, explain your decision by using evidence from pages 32–37.

▲ An engraving by Samuel Begg showing the scene in the House of Lords just after the peers voted to limit their own powers forever. The image appeared in *The Rise of the Democracy* by Joseph Clayton published in 1911

▲ Wentworth House, Yorkshire, 1893

Growing unrest

This may look like a ceremonial cavalry inspection in front of a royal palace, but something much more serious is happening. The building, Wentworth House, is twice as wide as Buckingham Palace. It belonged to the Fitzwilliams, a landowning family in south Yorkshire who became immensely rich in the nineteenth century when coal was found underneath their fields and woods.

Their great wealth enabled them to build this house, but it also brought them into conflict with the miners. In 1893, when this photograph was taken, the miners were on strike and attacking property, so the cavalry were called out to protect the mine-owning Fitzwilliams.

Deepening fear

Industrial strife worsened in the early twentieth century, reaching a peak in the years 1910 to 1914. In 1912 King George V felt that the danger of disorder, even revolution, was so great that he cancelled a foreign visit and wrote to Winston Churchill, the Home Secretary, asking whether law and order could be maintained. Churchill replied that it could, but probably not without people being killed. They both knew that several European governments had been overthrown by revolutions in the nineteenth century; there had been a revolution in Russia in 1905 during which it had looked as though the Tsar would lose his throne.

The fear of serious unrest in Britain in 1912 was so great that gunsmiths in London ran out of revolvers, as worried people armed themselves. The *Daily Mail* warned that

> The country is in a dangerous state of social disturbance … (this is) the opening phase of a real and irreparable class war.

As troops were called out in several areas, this socialist leaflet appeared:

> Men! Comrades! Brothers! You are in the Army. So are we. You, in the Army of Destruction. We are in the army of construction.
>
> We work at mine, mill, forge, factory or dock, producing and transporting all the goods, clothing, foodstuffs etc which makes it possible for people to live.
>
> You are Working men's Sons.
>
> When we go on strike to better our lot, which is also the lot of Your Fathers, Mothers, Brothers and Sisters, YOU are called upon by your officers to MURDER us. Don't do it.

Calling on soldiers to refuse to obey orders was treason. Whoever published this leaflet could be shot as a traitor. Clearly there were socialists in Britain who were so committed to bringing about deep and lasting change that they would risk their lives to make it happen.

Trade unions

The conflicts that so worried the king, the newspapers and members of ruling classes and that sometimes involved violence with troops on the streets, arose from a series of major strikes led by new-style trade unions.

During the nineteenth century, in the early years of the Industrial Revolution, workers soon realised that they had no rights at work. If an individual complained about wages, hours or conditions he or she would simply be sacked. But if large numbers of workers complained and, as a last resort, went on strike, the employer had to listen if only to keep the business going.

Trade unions were formed to organise this mass strength and to ensure their members had fair wages and fair working conditions – normally by negotiation but by calling a strike if negotiations broke down. At first only skilled workers formed successful unions: they had the power to shut down the factory and had enough wages to pay a union subscription. Unskilled workers were usually too poor and too easily sacked to join a union. One event that helped to change this was the London Dock Strike of 1889, as a result of which the unskilled workers on London docks won a pay increase. Three men emerged as leaders of that strike and went on to play an important part in militant trade union activity later: John Burns, Ben Tillett and Tom Mann.

All three were socialist trade unionists, but Burns and Tillett sought to improve the lives of working people through politics. Both became MPs, Burns as a Liberal and Tillett (for a while) in the Labour Party. Mann took a different route. When the Conservative government made difficulties for trade unions Mann went to Australia for ten years, returning to Britain in 1910 as a convinced syndicalist.

▲ John Burns, c. 1900

Syndicalism

Syndicalists argued that trying to improve the lives of working people through political action was a waste of time. They believed that the political system was in the hands of the middle and upper classes and geared to their interests, and that only trade unions really represented working people. Syndicalists argued that mass trade unions should act together in a general strike of millions of workers. This would bring the country to a halt, and the workers would take over the country's industries, by-passing the political system to set up a socialist state.

Not many trade unionists were whole-hearted syndicalists, but the idea had influence. An important pamphlet, 'The Miners' Next Step' was published in 1912, calling on the Miners' Union to take over running the coal mines. As we've seen, many trade unions were luke-warm in their support for the early Labour Party. They saw militant union activity as the best way of helping their working members.

▲ Ben Tillett, c. 1900

▲ Tom Mann speaking to strikers in Liverpool, 1911

Reflect

British governments were very worried by syndicalists even though there were very few of them. What might explain this?

Militant strikes and the 'Great Unrest'

▲ Police escorting strike breakers through Liverpool during the transport strike of 1911

Trade union membership increased from 1.6 million in 1911 to 2.7 million by 1914 – nearly 20 per cent of all workers. The unions started their own newspaper, the *Daily Herald*, to make their case to the public. The growing strength of the trade union movement and the tough attitudes of the leaders they elected, was a response to a demand for a better standard of living in the face of rising food prices. Between 1906 and 1910 food prices had risen by 25 per cent. For workers barely living on their wages, this was serious.

Many historians have labelled these years as the 'Great Unrest'. From 1910 onwards there were strikes in the docks, mills and shipyards, and a violent strike of transport workers in Dublin. There was even a school strike, at Burston in Norfolk, where the pupils went on strike in protest at the sacking of their teachers. In mid-1912 there were seventeen separate strikes in Lancashire alone.

The miners, who had been moderate 'Lib-Labs' in 1900, had become particularly militant by 1910. At Tonypandy, in south Wales, during the south Wales miners' strike of 1910–11, strikers clashed with police, with hand-to-hand fighting in the streets. A three-day riot broke out and Winston Churchill, as Home Secretary, sent in two companies of infantry and two hundred cavalry.

In Liverpool, seamen on strike in 1911 were supported by other transport workers led by Ben Tillett and Tom Mann, and the railwaymen.

As the meat in the unloaded ships began to stink, butter turned rancid and vegetables rotted, the strikers took control of the streets. Naval gunboats were sent to the River Mersey and mounted soldiers were sent into the city to keep order. Fighting went on for several days and two workers were shot. Tom Mann was arrested and served a prison sentence.

National Miners' Strike, 1912

In 1912 the million members of the miners' unions were on strike for 'fives and twos': 5s (25p) per shift for a man, 2s (10p) for a boy. Boys as young as twelve worked down the pits. John Cairns, a Northumberland miner, expressed the mix of frustration at their treatment by the mine-owners and their aspirations for a better life:

> Our men have been under the thumbs of the masters from at least 1870 until now and they desire better homes, better food, better clothing, better conditions.

As the supply of coal stopped, British industry began to grind to a halt. Asquith, the Prime Minister, broke into tears as he called on Parliament to grant the wage increase the miners were calling for.

Over 40 million working days were lost through strikes in 1912. In 1914 the 'Triple Alliance' was made, between the Miners, the Transport Workers (which covered seamen, dockers, and tram, bus and lorry-drivers) and the Railwaymen. Together, they had the power to bring the country to a halt – and their leaders knew it. Later that year, when Britain went to war, the trade unions had the ideal opportunity to bring down the government with a general strike of all union workers but their leaders chose not to and turned their members' efforts to fighting in the army or keeping Britain's industry running in a time of national crisis. There were strikes during the war years but none got out of control.

▲ English miners on strike in May 1912. The graffiti on the fence shows their determination to get the pay increase they were demanding

Historians' views

The years between 1910 and 1914 certainly saw serious industrial unrest in Britain, but historians disagree about just how serious these troubles were. Here are two examples.

An extract from an article on the website of the Internationalist Communist Tendency at www.leftcom.org viewed in 2016.

From 1910 to 1914 Britain was wracked by a series of strikes that were noted for their militancy. This militancy shook the British capitalist state to its foundations and forced the Liberal government of Herbert Henry Asquith to increasingly turn to military means in an attempt to halt the strikes.

An extract from *The Fateful Year – England 1914* by the historian Mark Bostridge, 2014.

Although there was widespread and genuine concern about the spread of industrial militancy, fanned by syndicalist ideas of class warfare and a general strike, in reality the notion of a giant formation of unions holding the country to ransom was something of a bluff.

Reflect

How do these two interpretations differ and what might explain any differences?

Record

Under the heading 'The challenge from militant labour,' make your final 'continuum chart' (see page 27). Tick the circle that you think best shows how great was the threat to political stability from militant labour groups between 1900 and 1914. Underneath this, explain your decision by using evidence from pages 38–41.

Review

You may have noticed that our enquiry title is taken from the first of the two interpretations above. The writer was concentrating on the years 1910–14 when he or she suggested that the British state was shaken to its foundations. If someone suggested that the same words could describe the whole period 1900–1914, how far would you agree with them? Explain your answer carefully, using your continuum charts to help you.

'The Welsh Wizard'

David Lloyd George is a key figure in this book. As you have seen in Enquiry 2, he was the radical Chancellor of the Exchequer who fought to introduce state support for the old, the ill and unemployed, and weakened for ever the power of the House of Lords. As you will discover in Enquiry 5, he was the dynamic Prime Minister who energised Britain to victory in the First World War.

His life

He was born in 1863 in Manchester, plain David George, the son of a teacher. But his father died and his mother returned to live near her family in north Wales when he was just two years old. He always called himself a proud Welshman.

He went to his local school unlike the rich public school and Oxbridge-educated Englishmen who dominated British politics in this period. His uncle, Richard Lloyd, encouraged him to train as a solicitor and then go into local politics. David even took on his name, calling himself David Lloyd George.

His early years in politics were spent as a Welsh nationalist Liberal, and he became a leading figure in *Cymru Fydd* (Young Wales). He developed a lasting dislike of the privileges of the Church of England; the power of the English upper classes, who he called simply 'The Dukes'; and wealthy English landowners.

He was elected to Parliament as a Liberal in 1890. Aged 27, he was the youngest MP and he was only 45 when he became Chancellor of the Exchequer.

He became Prime Minister in 1916 when he split his own Liberal Party by agreeing to lead a coalition (joint) government with Conservative support. He led Britain through the last years of the war, making difficult decisions on matters of life and death. After achieving victory in 1918, his coalition government continued for a while after the war. In that time he:

- took part in the peace-making negotiations at Versailles
- put through the Representation of the People Act, giving votes to (some) women
- passed a Housing Act, leading to the building of the first council houses
- passed a Rent Act, preventing big rent increases
- doubled the old age pension
- extended National Insurance to most workers
- sold peerages to anyone wealthy enough to donate £50,000 to Liberal or Conservative party funds.

In 1922 he lost his place as Prime Minister when the Conservatives abandoned him and he had

▲ Lloyd George, c. 1911

to resign. Although he remained an MP for 23 more years, he never held power again.

His skills as a speaker came from listening to the powerful sermons preached in the Non-Conformist chapels which most of the people of Wales supported. He loved to address enormous audiences often in open-air meetings. In 1980, the Labour MP Jennie Lee recalled how her father told her that: *'when Lloyd George came to address meetings you had to hold on to your seat not to be carried away'.*

His nickname 'The Welsh Wizard' was used in his lifetime. It may refer to his ability to cast a spell on audiences as he spoke or to his apparently magical ability to achieve almost impossible changes in society in stormy and difficult circumstances.

His private life was full of controversy. In 1888 he had married Margaret Owen, the daughter of a Welsh farmer, with whom he had five children, two of whom also became MPs. But in 1913 he began an affair with his secretary, Frances Stevenson, which lasted for the rest of his life. Margaret died in 1941 and he married Frances in 1943, two years before his own death. This, and his many other affairs, explain his other nickname: 'The Goat'. This was originally given him by a civil servant who was astonished at Lloyd George's appetite for government paperwork, but it was used by his enemies to refer to his appetite for sex. Rumours also circulated that he was involved in corrupt deals that added to his own wealth.

His reputation

Historians have disagreed in the assessment of Lloyd George and his career. Some see him as a remarkably effective leader with many proud achievements. Others see him as a deceitful hypocrite who split his own party and allowed the Labour Party to take over from the Liberals as rivals to the Conservatives.

There are all sorts of reasons why we should not be surprised that historians have interpreted his career so differently:

- His long career involved him in many complex and controversial changes that stir up strong opinions.
- He published his own, very long political memoirs that give historians far more sources to work with than they have for other politicians.
- Some historians are more ready than others to overlook his affairs, his sale of peerages and rumours of corruption.
- His speeches often made sweeping promises that he failed to carry out in practice so it is hard to decide what he really believed or wanted.
- His values, such as his open support for the British Empire, are not widely shared in recent times.

His statue

In 2007, this statue of Lloyd George was unveiled in Parliament Square at Westminster. Historians share their views with words and paper but the sculptor, Glynn Williams, has shown us his own interpretation of Lloyd George in metal and stone. You may be able to relate each of these features of the statue to something from the summary of Lloyd George's life that you have just read:

- The figure steps forwards into a powerful wind as he holds his hat in his hand and his cape blows behind him.
- His hand gestures forwards and towards the Houses of Parliament.
- He stands firmly fixed on an enormous, solid block of Welsh slate.
- He is shown as being about 55, when he was at the peak of his career.
- He is located next to the statue of Winston Churchill, Britain's successful leader in the Second World War.

Controversy

The unveiling of the statue in 2007 caused great controversy. Protestors angrily insisted that it should never have been allowed. Their objection was that Lloyd George had ordered the bombing of Iraq during the First World War when it was ruled by the Turks who were allies of Germany. In 2007, British troops

▲ A statue of Lloyd George in Parliament Square, London, c. 2007

were again fighting a war in Iraq, having invaded the country alongside American forces in 2003. The protesters argued that it was adding insult to injury for innocent Iraqis who were once again suffering at the hands of western imperial powers.

Maybe, if the statue had been set up a few years earlier it would all have passed off in peace. This is a fine example of how interpretations of the past are influenced by events in the present.

3

Fighting against the tide

Why had women not won the vote by 1914?

▲ The 'Lands End to London' route of the 1913 'Suffrage Pilgrimage'

This photograph shows a group of women as they set off on a 300-mile bicycle journey from Land's End to London. As you can see from their banner, the women belonged to the National Union of Suffrage Societies known as suffragists. In August 1913, thousands of suffragists travelled from different parts of Britain and converged on London for a mass protest in Hyde Park. The women were taking part in a peaceful campaign for the right to vote (suffrage).

Today, all British citizens over the age of eighteen have the right to vote, but the situation was very different at the beginning of the twentieth century. By 1900 all men over 21 who owned property or who paid sufficient rent had been granted the right to vote, but this was still denied to women. From the end of the nineteenth century, the suffragists slowly gained support from different sections of society, including from many MPs.

In 1903 Emmeline Pankhurst, frustrated by the slow progress of the campaign for female suffrage, formed the Women's Social and Political Union. Members of the WSPU, known as suffragettes, campaigned more actively for the vote. This famous photograph shows the arrest of their leader Emmeline Pankhurst for chaining herself to the railings outside Buckingham Palace on 21 May 1914. She and other suffragettes were trying to present George V with a petition demanding the right to vote for women. The police officer carried Emmeline to a waiting car which took her to Holloway prison.

▶ A photograph of the arrest of Emmeline Pankhurst, 21 May 1914

The Enquiry

As you will discover in this enquiry, the campaign for women to have the vote took many forms. However, despite all the campaigning, women still did not have the right to vote by the time war broke out in 1914. In this enquiry you will investigate the different ways in which women campaigned for the vote and explain why their aim was so difficult to achieve.

You will learn about:

● Women's lives at the beginning of the twentieth century
● The different campaigns for the vote and the opposition they faced
● The government and changes in the campaigns, 1910–1914.

As you read each section of this enquiry, you should make three 'factor sheets' to explain why women had not won the vote by 1914.

Public attitudes	Campaigning methods	Political responses

Women's lives c. 1900

In 1900 the widely-held view of men and women was that they lived in separate spheres. Men were out in the world, taking part in politics and public life. Many people thought that this was a tough world to which a woman's gentle nature was not suited. Women were seen as less rational and more emotional than men, and were thought to be better suited to the private world of home and family. At the beginning of the twentieth century, many people thought that women did not need to vote as their husband could vote for them.

Women and the family

Families differed then as much as now, and we should not assume that all women were unhappy with their lives. However, women were certainly much more restricted than they are now, and this was true at all levels of society.

Upper- and middle-class women

Upper- and middle-class women often had quite easy lives, but the gender divide was very strong and women were excluded from most careers and from public life. It was, as one woman said 'a life of leisure, not freedom'. A woman was expected to be 'the angel of the house', creating an orderly and attractive home for her husband. Edwardian Britain was a patriarchal society. Men were in charge; wives were expected to do as they were told by their husbands.

Edwardian upper-class women often had very little to do. Small children were looked after by a nanny who would present the child to the mother in the early evening so that they could spend an hour two together. At the age of seven or eight, children were sent away to boarding school and mothers would only see their children during school holidays. Upper-class women were certainly not expected to do any work in the house. They had a large number of servants who would do all the cooking and cleaning, and who would help them dress and take a bath.

In some middle-class families there were signs of change. Families were smaller and marriage, at least in some cases, was seen as more of a partnership. Some women found an outlet for their talents in voluntary work for the Church and for charities. However, there was still a general expectation that a middle-class woman would devote herself to her husband and would focus on looking after the home. With at

▲ A middle-class Edwardian family in their garden, c. 1905

least one servant to do the housework, many middle-class married women had little to occupy them. It was mainly women of this class who took part in the campaign for the vote.

Working-class women

Life for working-class women remained hard. Couples usually married in their mid-20s, having saved some money to furnish their first home, and from then until well into her 50s, a woman was fully occupied with child-rearing and house-keeping. Although the average number of children in a family had decreased from around six or seven in 1800 to four or five in 1900, many families were much larger. One Edwardian working-class mother stated:

I am the mother of eleven children — six girls and five boys. I was only 19 years old when my first baby was born ... for twenty years I was always feeding or expecting babies.

In the early 1900s it was expected that working-class women would do all the jobs in the house, with the help of their daughters when they were old enough. Without any of today's labour-saving devices, such as washing machines, vacuum cleaners or electric cookers, these tasks involved endless hard toil. A Durham miner's wife recalled:

> Monday was my easy day — I tidied the house, sorted and soaked clothes for Tuesday's wash, sewed buttons and darned socks. Tuesday I washed. Ironed on the Wednesday because we had lines up all around the house and we had to wait until the clothes dried. I'd do all the rooms Thursday. Friday was my baking day. Cleaning the windows and outdoor jobs were done on a Saturday.

Maud Pember Reeves, a member of the London Fabian Society, carried out a detailed survey of women's lives in Lambeth and published her findings in 1913 under the title *Round about a pound a week.* You will remember from reading about Rowntree's work in Enquiry 1 how significant this sum was – not enough to keep a family above the poverty line. The task of careful budgeting, endlessly watching the pennies, was the woman's. Below was a typical working day for Mrs T, a mother of six children. They lived in two rooms on the first floor in a house with water only available from a tap in the yard downstairs. Mrs T's husband did not like eating with the family, so ate his meals separately.

▲ Young girls helping with the washing in the East End of London, 1912

6.00 Feeds baby
6.30 Gets up, calls five children, puts kettle on stove, washes smaller children and dresses them, does the hair of the three girls
7.30 Gets husband's breakfast
8.00 Gives him breakfast alone, feeds baby, cuts bread and dripping for children's breakfast
8.30 Husband leaves for work, children leave for school; she has her own breakfast
9.00 Clears away and washes up
9.30 Carries slops downstairs, carries buckets of water upstairs
10.00 Washes and dresses baby, feeds him
11.00 Sweeps bedroom, scrubs stairs and passage
12.00 Goes shopping for the day's food
12.15 Children home for lunch
12.30 Cooks and lays lunch
1.00 Gives children lunch, feeds baby
1.45 Washes children, sends them back to school
2.00 Washes up from lunch, scrubs kitchen, cleans grate, empties dirty water, fetches more water from yard
3.00 Feeds baby
3.30 Mends clothes
4.30 Children home from school. Gets their tea
5.00 Clears away, washes up, feeds baby, does more mending
6.30 Cooks husband's tea
7.00 Husband eats tea
7.30 Puts younger children to bed
8.00 Tidies up, washes up husband's tea things, sweeps kitchen, mends clothes, feeds baby, puts older children to bed
8.45 Gets husband's supper
10.00 Feeds baby and settles for the night
10.30 Goes to bed

Reflect

Why do you think it was difficult for a working-class woman to join the campaign for the vote?

Women's work

Although two-thirds of twenty-year-old women worked, marriage, and certainly the arrival of the first child, put an end to that. Only one in twenty married women worked. This was partly because of the time it took to run a home without modern technology, but it was also a matter of male pride: a man was shamed if his wife had to go out to work. In addition, many trade unions were strongly opposed to women working. The unions were afraid that women would be paid less and that this would deprive men of jobs or drive down men's wages. A speaker at a trade union conference told the audience:

> It is your duty as men and husbands to use your utmost efforts to bring about a condition of things where wives would be in their proper sphere at home, instead of being dragged into competition with the great and strong men of the world.

Jobs at all levels, from most professions such as law to the better-paid working-class jobs such as engine-drivers and boilermakers, excluded women. Most workplaces were entirely male environments. However, there were exceptions to this pattern: women, including married women, had always worked in the Potteries and in the Lancashire cotton mills.

In cotton-weaving areas, working together, belonging to a trade union, and having their own money gave women in these areas an independence which led to their playing a big part in the campaign for the vote.

Reflect

Which factors made it unlikely that many working-class women would join the women's suffrage campaign?

▼ Women weavers at a cotton mill in Lancashire, early 1900s

Elsewhere, women's lives were more restricted. They could only hope to earn a few pennies by washing clothes or by doing piece work at home, as in the photo below.

◄ A woman and her daughter making hair-brushes at home in the East End of London, early 1900s

New opportunities, but limitations

The twentieth century brought some new opportunities for women's work. With compulsory free education for all children, there were many more schools, and Florence Nightingale had successfully made nursing a respectable career. By 1900 there were 172,000 women teachers and 64,000 nurses. Local government had expanded, creating office jobs for women. The growth of high street shops and department stores created a demand for female shop-assistants. Although the hours were very long – often 80 hours a week – these jobs were seen as preferable to the demeaning job of being a servant or working in a dirty factory.

Despite these new opportunities, the barriers for Edwardian women were still high and employment was very unequal. While male teachers were paid £127 a year, female teachers were paid £92. The professions were still largely closed to women. Alongside all those female teachers and nurses there were just 277 female doctors, 6 architects, 3 vets, 2 accountants – and no lawyers. The biggest single type of job for women in 1900 remained domestic service, employing nearly 2 million women.

◄ Women typists in an office, 1912. Early typewriters were not much like the modern computer, and typists were subject to strict discipline

Reflect

How was women's work beginning to change in Edwardian times?

In what ways were employment opportunities still limited for Edwardian women?

Record

Add some points to your first factor sheet on 'public attitudes' to explain why it was difficult for women to campaign for the vote.

Campaigns for the vote

The campaign for votes for women grew out of a much wider movement for women's equality in the nineteenth century. Radical women were concerned about a whole range of issues – unequal divorce laws, health, education, poor pay. It became clear that many of these issues needed changes in the law and yet women were in no position to influence law-making. The need for female suffrage led to Women's Suffrage Societies being formed in many towns and cities. Their case included matters of principle and practicality:

● Laws should reflect the wishes of all the people. It is a democratic principle that those who live under the law should have a say in how laws are made.
● Parliament makes laws affecting women's work, homes, children and education; these are issues in which women have particular interest and experience.
● Women had shown that they were perfectly able to play a part in political life as thousands worked as volunteers for political parties at election time.
● Women had already shown that they could play an active and responsible part in public life. By 1900 women could stand for election to school boards and as Poor Law Guardians. There were 270 women school board members and 1546 women Poor Law Guardians by 1900.

▼ Millicent Fawcett, c. 1895

◀ An NUWSS badge

The Suffragists

In 1897 the network of local Women's Suffrage Societies joined together in a national organisation – the National Union of Women's Suffrage Societies (NUWSS). In 1900 Millicent Fawcett was elected President.

Millicent Fawcett was married to a Liberal MP and was the sister of Elizabeth Garrett Anderson, the first Englishwoman to qualify as a doctor. Millicent was a tireless speaker, writer and organiser.

The NUWSS was a non-party organisation and included members from right across the political spectrum. The NUWSS had its roots in Victorian Liberalism (although Millicent Fawcett started as a Conservative). There were many Liberal members as well as some socialists who were members of the Independent Labour Party (ILP) and the Labour Party.

Name	National Union of Women's Suffrage Societies (NUWSS)
Known as	Suffragists
Date began	1897 as a national organisation, with many local suffrage societies formed much earlier
President/leader	Millicent Fawcett
Support	Nationwide, mainly middle-class but with considerable working-class support, especially in north-west England
Aims	Giving the vote to women on the same terms as men
Strategy	To influence public opinion through any legal means: pamphlets, posters, marches, rallies
Tactics	To support any MP, of any party, who promised to support their aims

The Suffragettes

▼ Emmeline Pankhurst

Emmeline Pankhurst was a member of the ILP in Manchester and campaigned for equal rights for women. She became exasperated with the failure of the NUWSS to achieve its aims and in 1903 formed a breakaway organisation, the Women's Social and Political Union (WSPU).

Emmeline Pankhurst and her daughters, particularly Christabel and Sylvia, were the centre of the suffragette movement. She moved the WSPU to London in 1906 to carry on the campaign, leaving her left-wing roots behind. At first the two organisations campaigned together, but key differences in strategy and tactics soon emerged between them. Most famously, WSPU members were prepared to take much more militant action, including breaking the law, to keep the issue of the vote in the headlines. 'Deeds not Words' was their motto.

Emmeline was no quiet organiser like Millicent Fawcett. She was prepared to get arrested, even to go to prison, where she went on hunger strike many times. She had the ability to arouse fanatical support from her followers.

The WSPU was largely a middle- and upper-class organisation, whose members included titled aristocrats. One of the few working-class suffragettes was Annie Kenney, who had worked in a cotton mill from the age of thirteen and had her finger torn off in one of the machines. She threw herself into the life of the WSPU, left her family, moved to London and later joined the Pankhursts. At 21 she was campaigning full-time and later described this life in her autobiography:

◀ A WSPU badge

> The changed life into which most of us entered was a revolution in itself. No home life, no one to say what we should do or what we should not do, no family ties, we were free and alone in a great brilliant city, scores of young women scarcely out of their teens met together in a revolutionary movement, outlaws or breakers of laws, independent of everything and everybody, fearless and self-confident … It was an unwritten rule that there should be no concerts, no theatres, no smoking; work, and sleep to prepare us for more work, was the unwritten order of the day.

Name	Women's Social and Political Union (WSPU)
Known as	Suffragettes
Date began	1903
President/leader	Emmeline Pankhurst
Support	Nationwide, but increasingly based in London
Aims	To win the vote for women on the same basis as men (i.e. the same as the NUWSS)
Strategy	To put pressure on the government – which from 1906 meant the Liberals – to pass a law giving the vote to women (i.e. the same as the NUWSS)
Tactics	To harass Liberal MPs and ministers; to break the law if necessary to get publicity for their cause

Reflect

What did these two organisations have in common? How did they differ?

Which of these two organisations do you think would be most effective in persuading politicians and the public?

The Suffragette campaign, 1905–09

In 1905, Christabel Pankhurst and Annie Kenney were the first suffragettes to be arrested. They had gone to a meeting in Manchester addressed by a Liberal government minister and kept calling out *'Will the Liberal government give votes for women?'*. Christabel refused to stop and the police were called to take her out of the meeting. In the ensuing struggle she was alleged to have spat at a policeman. She was later fined 5 shillings (25p) but refused to pay the fine, so was sent to prison for a week. This event caused a huge public furore. That a woman – a middle-class woman – should do such a thing was considered outrageous and seized all the newspaper headlines.

The Pankhursts took the view that any publicity was good publicity and from 1907 escalated their law-breaking, courting arrest. Chaining themselves to the railings of Buckingham Palace, for example, soon brought the police to arrest them.

▼ Christabel Pankhurst in Manchester in 1909, shortly after her release from Holloway prison

The impact of the Suffragette campaign

- They were highly successful in winning publicity: 'Votes for women' filled the pages of newspapers. New members joined, and money poured in.
- The suffragette colours of white, purple and green could be seen everywhere, on badges and banners, as well as all kinds of items such as tea services and brooches.
- However, there was a reaction to their publicity-seeking violence: many supporters of votes for women who disapproved of the suffragettes' methods joined the NUWSS, whose membership grew and grew, always far outnumbering the WSPU.
- The big crowds at WSPU meetings did not necessarily mean huge support. Many seem to have turned up to mock, and speakers sometimes had to be rescued by the police.

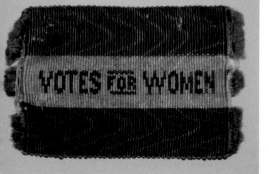

▲ A suffragette badge c. 1907

Reflect

What were the successes and the failures of this stage of the WSPU campaign?

Opposition

Opposition based on attitudes like those demonstrated in this poster was common. At meetings and rallies suffragette speakers were often told to *'Go home and darn your husband's socks!'*

The National Anti-Suffrage League was formed in 1910. It was well funded and by 1910 had 9000 members and over 80 branches. Their main arguments were:

- Men and women had 'separate spheres'.
- Women's views were already heard through their influence in the home, on men and through public opinion.
- Women could already take part in elections to local government. This was quite enough for their limited time and energies, given that they had homes to run and families to look after.
- Women were not required to fight for their country, so should not have a say in its government.

Reflect

How does this poster oppose the suffragettes?

▲ A poster opposing the suffragettes

Politicians' responses

Persuading an all-male Parliament to give votes to women was a challenging task, but it was made more difficult because elements within the campaign for women's suffrage had different aims.

Remember that the right to vote was property-based; it lay with heads of households and property-owners or those who paid sufficient rent, which meant that around four in ten men could not vote. What exactly should women demand: the right to vote on the same property-basis as men, or votes for all men and women?

Reflect

Until as late as 1912, none of the parties adopted votes for women as their official programme. Why not?

Votes for women on the same basis as men: a property-based franchise

- Supported by WSPU and most of NUWSS: this would be the simplest change and would give the vote to lots more women.
- Some members of the NUWSS firmly opposed this because it would still leave working class women and men without the vote.
- Some Liberals supported votes for women, but leading Liberals (including Asquith, Prime Minister from 1908) opposed it. They feared that this would give the vote to middle- and upper-class women – mainly Conservative voters.
- Labour Party was split: many were against it as it would not help working class men or women.
- Attractive to Conservatives, but they were in opposition after 1906.

Votes for all men and women: full adult suffrage

- Opposed by most Liberals as far too big a change; anyway would not get through the House of Lords.
- Also opposed by all Conservatives as too big a change and one which would bring more votes to Liberals and Labour.
- Some radical members of the NUWSS campaigned hard for this target
- Although some influential members of the Labour Party, including Keir Hardie, supported it, the Party was split as many were campaigning primarily for the vote for all men. Many argued that to include women in their demand would make it even less likely to be achievable.

Record

Add some points from pages 50–53 to each of your three factor sheets.

The government and changes in the campaigns, 1910–1914

An ordinary MP can introduce a bill (a proposal to make a law) about a topic which he or she thinks is important. These are called Private Members' Bills and usually they stand no chance of becoming law unless the government picks up the issue and gives it Parliamentary time. From the end of the nineteenth century Private Members' Bills for giving women the vote were regularly put before Parliament. In 1908 the majority of MPs voted for the bill as you can see in the table below, but without support from Asquith's Liberal government the bill could not become law.

	Conservatives	Liberals	Irish	Labour	TOTAL
For	30	185	21	33	269
Against	30	48	14	2	94

However, without support from the government the bill could not become law. As you know, Asquith's Liberal government was more concerned with introducing its new social reforms, and Asquith himself feared that giving women the vote on the same basis as men would disadvantage the Liberals in elections. In the years after 1910, the campaigners for women's suffrage became frustrated by the lack of government response. Some Suffragettes turned to violence.

▼ 'Black Friday', 18 November 1910

In 1910 . . .

. . . another Private Members' Bill to give women the vote was introduced and was getting plenty of support when Asquith refused to give it any more time. The suffragettes were furious and called for an anti-Liberal demonstration.

On Friday 18 November, fighting broke out with the police in London, which lasted for six hours. Asquith's car was damaged and there were 115 arrests. One suffragette described how she was treated by the police:

> Several times constables and plain-clothes men who were in the crowds passed their arms round me from the back and clutched hold of my breasts in as public a manner as possible, and men in the crowd followed their example … My skirt was lifted up as high as possible, and the constable attempted to lift me off the ground by raising his knee. This he could not do, so he threw me into the crowd and incited the men to treat me as they wished.

In 1911 . . .

. . . another bill to give votes to women won support when Asquith suddenly announced that he would bring in a bill to give 'manhood suffrage' (votes for all men). He suggested that an amendment could be added to the bill to include some women on the same basis as men: those who were not married but met the property-owning qualification in their own right. This would have given the vote to about 1 million women: rich widows and unmarried women.

Asquith's cynical approach caused dismay and anger across the women's campaign. The suffragettes understandably felt they had been out-manoeuvred and betrayed by the Liberal government. In 1912 the suffragettes stepped up their violent actions with renewed vigour.

- There was series of window-smashing raids across Britain. Many shops were attacked on the high streets of towns and cities. In London, militant suffragettes also smashed the windows of government buildings.
- There were arson attacks on postboxes, theatres, MPs' houses and sporting pavilions.
- Some of the more extreme suffragettes even began to place bombs in and outside banks, churches and other buildings.

The newspapers often referred to the attacks as 'outrages' and suggested that the suffragettes were terrorising their own society.

◀ Window-smashing in London, 1911

An extract from an article by Fern Riddell in *History Today*, March 2015

The year 1912 saw an ever increasing escalation of violence among militant suffragettes. Glasgow Art Gallery had its glass cases smashed; bank and post office windows were smashed from Kew to Gateshead; in September, 23 trunk telegraph wires were cut on the London Road at Potters Bar and on November 28th simultaneous attacks on post boxes occurred across the entire country. By the end of the year, 240 people had been sent to prison for militant suffragette activities. The newspapers began to carry weekly round-ups of the attacks, with the Gloucester Journal and the Liverpool Echo running dedicated columns to report on the latest outrages. In early 1913 a suffragette attacked the glass cabinets in the Tower of London's Jewel House, while in Dundee, four postmen were severely injured by phosphorus chemicals left in post boxes. In Dumbarton 20 telegraph wires were cut; Kew Gardens orchid house was attacked and its tea house burnt down.

In 1912 . . .

. . . another bill for votes for women was defeated by just fourteen votes. This time 73 Liberals, MPs and nearly all the Irish MPs voted against the bill as they wanted Parliament to get on with their big issue: Home Rule for Ireland.

	Conservatives	Liberals	Irish	Labour	TOTAL
For	63	117	3	35	**218**
Against	114	73	35	–	**222**

Violence escalated still further as you can read in the extract on the right.

Record

Add more points to your three factor sheets.

Hunger strikes

The increase in militant action after 1910 resulted in many suffragettes being sent to prison. Imprisoned suffragettes argued that they should have the status of political prisoners. This would have given them certain privileges such as more frequent visits and the freedom to write books and articles. The government refused their demand. From 1909, the imprisoned suffragettes began to use hunger strikes in protest. The prison authorities, anxious to avoid the deaths of suffragettes in custody, began the practice of force-feeding the hunger-striking women through a tube. This was a brutal procedure that caused intense pain and could endanger the women's health. Emmeline Pankhurst, who went on hunger strike in Holloway prison, London, was horrified by the screams of the women during force-feeding. In her autobiography, she wrote: *'Holloway became a place of horror and torment. Sickening scenes of violence took place almost every hour of the day, as the doctors went from cell to cell performing their hideous office'*.

▼ Lady Constance Lytton, c. 1912

Lady Constance Lytton

One woman who endured the horror of force-feeding during her imprisonment at Walton gaol was Lady Constance Lytton. During earlier periods of imprisonment in London, Lytton had suspected that working-class suffragettes were treated more harshly than upper-class women like herself. She decided to test her theory by assuming the dress and name of a working woman, Jane Warton. She was arrested at a demonstration in Liverpool and was imprisoned in Walton gaol. She began a hunger strike, and, after four days, was fed by force.

On 18 January 1910, the Senior Medical Officer of the prison and five female prison officers entered Lytton's cell. They told her to lie on the plank bed. Two wardresses held her arms, one held her head and another held her feet; the fifth helped the doctor to pour the food. Lytton clenched her teeth tightly together, but the doctor forced them apart with a steel implement and fixed a steel gag in her mouth, opening the gag to force her jaws wide apart. He then inserted a four-foot tube down Lytton's throat and quickly poured in the liquid food. Lytton was instantly sick, but the wardress forced back her head and the force-feeding continued. She later wrote: *'the horror of it was more than I can describe'*. Lytton continued her hunger strike and endured another seven force-feedings before her release from Walton gaol at the end of January. She never really recovered from her ordeal, suffered a stroke in 1912, and died in 1923.

▼ An artist's impression of a suffragette being force-fed; published in the *Illustrated London News*, 27 April 1912

The government came in for considerable criticism over force-feeding. In response, after three and a half years of this brutal treatment, they passed the Prisoners' Temporary Discharge for Ill Health Act in 1913. Prisoners on hunger strike were released as soon as they became ill, then re-imprisoned when they had recovered. This Act was soon nicknamed the 'Cat and Mouse Act', as suffragettes were let go and then caught again, like mice being played with by a cat. This WSPU election poster makes the point well.

▼ WSPU poster, 1914

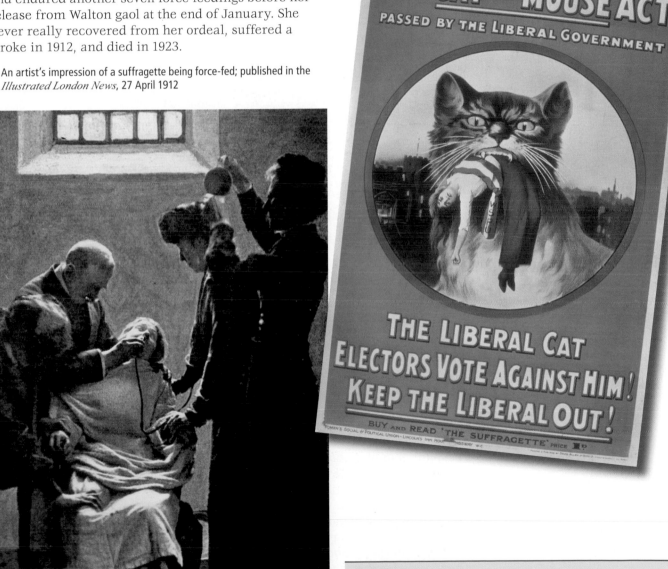

Record

On your 'Political responses' factor sheet explain how the Cat and Mouse Act limited the impact of the suffragettes' campaign.

Reflect

Emily Davison's action at the Derby was captured on film as well as in photographs. What effect do you think her death would have had on public opinion?

Changing support, 1913–14

In June 1913 a shocking event occurred which had an important impact on support for the suffragettes. Emily Wilding Davison had studied at Oxford University and was working as a teacher when she became utterly committed to the suffragette movement. She threw stones at Lloyd George's car, having wrapped the stones in her favourite words: '*Rebellion against tyrants is obedience to God.*' By June 1913 she was acting almost on her own, beyond the influence of the Pankhursts, so it is hard to know what she intended when she went to the world-famous Derby horse race at Epsom.

Emily made her way to the front of the crowd and stood by the rails next to the track. As the horses thundered round the corner she ducked under the rails and ran in front of the king's horse. The horse struck her and she was thrown to the ground. The photograph shows Emily Davison on the left. The jockey, who was seriously injured, lies on the right. Emily never recovered from her injuries and died in hospital four days later. Perhaps she intended to commit suicide, but most historians think that she was just trying to tie the suffragette colours to the king's horse.

▶ The scene at the June 1913 Derby moments after Emily Wilding Davison threw herself before the king's horse

Emmeline Pankhurst decided to make Emily Davison a martyr to the cause of female suffrage and her funeral a major WSPU event. From the hospital, four black horses pulled the funeral carriage, and six suffragettes, including Sylvia Pankhurst, marched alongside. The procession included 50 hunger strikers, some on release because of ill health, and hundreds of women ex-prisoners. An estimated 6000 women took part in the funeral service in London and more than 50,000 people turned out on the streets to watch the funeral pass by. The coffin was then taken to Emily Davison's home in Morpeth, Northumberland, where again huge crowds turned out the next day. However, the grief shown by the suffragettes was not shared widely by the British public. Many people were shocked that the tactics used to win the vote for women had become so extreme.

The WSPU and the NUWSS

By 1913, many people were becoming hostile to the whole idea of winning votes for women by using violent tactics and support for the WSPU was in decline. Sixty suffragettes were in prison and more were in hiding to avoid being re-arrested under the Cat and Mouse Act. There were perhaps 5000 members in some 80 branches, but public opinion was turning against them. Many influential members were leaving, unwilling to put up with the undemocratic way it was run by Emmeline Pankhurst, its lack of proper financial accounts and its fanatical arson campaign. Sylvia Pankhurst was increasingly unhappy with the direction of the WSPU. In 1913 she left to help form the East London Federation of Suffragettes (ELF), which combined socialism with a demand for women's suffrage.

The NUWSS, on the other hand, was flourishing. It made the most of its law-abiding policy as it stepped up its peaceful campaign. When the Labour Party decided to support votes for all men and women on an equal basis, the NUWSS abandoned its non-party policy and began to support Labour Party candidates at elections with money and volunteers. The suffragists continued to organise demonstrations and processions across Britain. By 1914 the NUWSS had around 50,000 members in some 500 branches.

◄ The Pilgrimage of August 1913 in Hyde Park. Millicent Fawcett is addressing the meeting and Selina Cooper (see page 60) is standing on the far left

When the First World War broke out in 1914 Emmeline Pankhurst decided that Britain needed the support of all its citizens and she persuaded the WSPU to stop its militant activities. It would be the hard work, resilience and bravery of British women during the war years which would finally persuade parliament to grant women over 30 the vote in 1918. In 1928 this was extended to all women over 21. Emmeline Pankhurst died just 18 days before the 1928 Act was passed.

Review

In his book *The Edwardians* published in 2004, Roy Hattersley wrote the following about the women's campaign for the vote:

'It was always going to be difficult, if not impossible, to defy the prejudices of a male-dominated society'

How far do you agree with Roy Hattersley's view of why women had not won the vote by 1914?

Record

Add some final points to your factor sheets.

The work of the historian Jill Liddington

◄ The historian, Jill Liddington

For much of the twentieth century, the story of women's campaign for the vote mainly focused on middle-class suffragettes in London. One historian has made it her life's work to tell some very different stories. In the 1970s, Jill Liddington began her research work on the only well-known working-class suffragette, Annie Kenney. She explains:

> I wanted to find out more about the suffragette Annie Kenney. I discovered that she had worked in the very mill next door to where I lived. I was set. In my mind, the campaigners now came from somewhere; they belonged somewhere. Whose other local stories could I unearth?

Selina Cooper

Just one of the remarkable women whose life Liddington has revealed is Selina Cooper. At the age of twelve, Selina was working part time as a winder in a cotton mill in Nelson, Lancashire. At thirteen she went full time, and was paid 8 shillings (40p) for a 56-hour week. She joined the Cotton Weavers' Union and soon made a name for herself by speaking for the

▲ Selina Cooper c. 1911

rights of women workers – to have doors on the toilets, for example. However, she found that the union was not interested, and was even actively hostile, to raising women's concerns.

Selina was aware how much she had missed in her education and began attending classes in Nelson run by the Co-operative Women's Guild. One of the main objectives of the Guild was to enable women to *discuss matters beyond the narrow confines of their domestic lives.'* Already committed to women's equality, she joined the ILP, where met and married Robert Cooper, a fellow socialist.

Selina stood as an ILP candidate for the Poor Law Board of Guardians and was elected, the first working-class woman to hold such a position. However, her main effort was in the campaign for women's suffrage, as a member of the North of England Society for Women's Suffrage, part of Mrs Fawcett's NUWSS. In 1900 she helped organise a petition of Lancashire women calling for the vote. Thirty thousand signatures were collected and she was chosen as one of the delegates to present the petition to Parliament. For the next few years Selina gained a reputation as a powerful speaker for women's rights. She addressed the Labour Party Conference in 1905 and Millicent Fawcett called on her regularly to speak at NUWSS rallies across Britain. She met Asquith, the Prime Minister, in 1910, and in 1912 was influential in persuading the NUWSS to support the Labour Party.

Selina Cooper had no time for the middle-class suffragettes of the WSPU: their aim to win the vote for women on the same basis as men was no use to women like her and she criticised their actions as *'playing for effects, not results.'* Selina had a child and a disabled mother to look after, and, like many of the northern working-class women suffragists, struggled to combine campaigning with family. Millicent Fawcett got the NUWSS to give her a small salary as a national organiser so that she could pay one of her friends as housekeeper when she was away for longer periods. Nevertheless, her daughter, born in 1900, recorded the menus she carefully wrote out before she went away and the postcards she always sent home.

Vanishing for the Vote

Jill Liddington's recent research has focused on the suffragette boycott of the 1911 census. The census aimed to record every person in every household on the night of 2 April 1911. Many suffragettes boycotted the census as a protest against not having the vote. They avoided the census in a variety of ways. Some camped out in the countryside, some drove cars around all night, some arranged mass sleepovers in secret attics. In Birmingham 120 women and 10 male supporters spent the night at the WSPU headquarters. Emily Wilding Davison hid in a cupboard in the Houses of Parliament. This photograph was taken at 3.30 a.m. at the Aldwych Skating Rink in London where around 500 women and 70 men evaded the census by attending an all-night protest meeting.

Some suffragettes stayed at home, but refused to fill in the census form. Jill Liddington researched the 1911 census forms which are stored at the National Archives and available online at www.nationalarchives.gov.uk. Below, you can see an example from the many which she found where women had written explanations of why they were refusing to complete the form.

In her book, *Vanishing for the Vote* Jill Liddington argued that the census boycott was an effective

▲ The census boycott at Aldwych Skating Rink, April 1911

protest. It is true that the impact on the overall population figures was very small, but that was not the boycotters' aim. They achieved plenty of publicity, with pictures and stories of the boycott on the front pages of several popular newspapers. It was a totally non-violent protest, making a strong point most effectively.

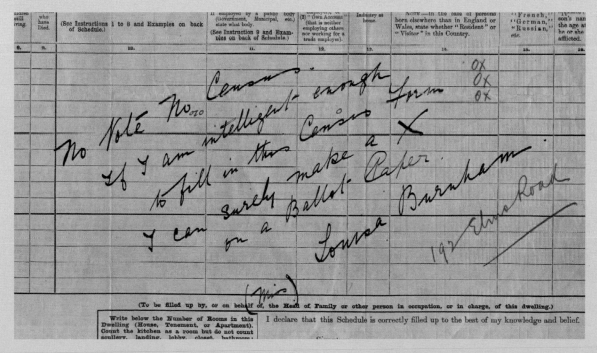

◀ Census return for Louisa Burnham, Clapham, London, April 1911

Jill Liddington's books include:

- *One Hand Tied Behind Us: Rise of the Women's Suffrage Movement*, 1978 (with Jill Norris)
- *Respectable Rebel: the life and times of Selina Cooper*, 1984
- *Rebel Girls*, 2006
- *Vanishing for the Vote*, 2014

Jill Liddington's work has not only changed views of the Votes for Women campaign and especially of the activities of the suffragists but has also revealed the remarkable lives of many ordinary women.

4

'The most beneficial empire'

How were British attitudes to the Empire changing?

▲ The Diamond Jubilee Procession, 1897

The British Empire in 1900 was the largest the world had ever seen, covering a quarter of the earth's land and containing a fifth of its population. At its head was the Queen Empress, Victoria. In 1897, Victoria celebrated her Diamond Jubilee with a magnificent procession through London. This photograph shows the Queen on her way to St Paul's Cathedral for a service of Thanksgiving. This procession included 50,000 British and Empire soldiers from all over the world.

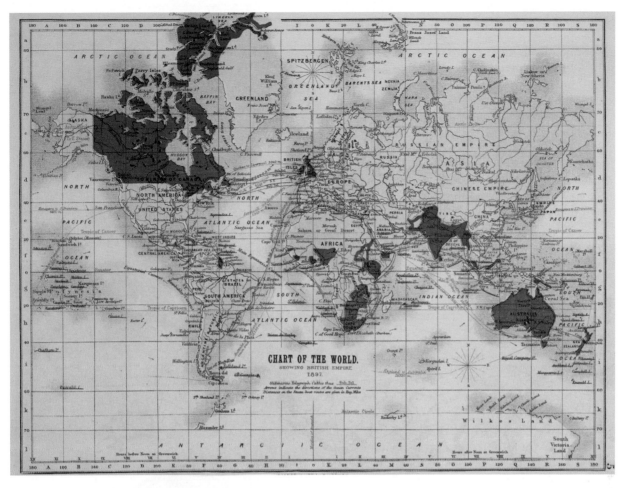

▲ The British Empire, 1897

The map above shows a world dominated by the British Empire at the beginning of the twentieth century. These were the great years of British Imperialism, when its expansion seemed unending, inevitable– and a force for good. British Imperialists liked to contrast the British Empire with earlier empires such as, Babylon, Egypt and Rome. These were seen as cruel tyrannies in comparison with the British Empire which a writer for *The Times* newspaper described as '*the most beneficial empire ever known*'.

But some people in Britain, and in parts of the empire, especially India and Ireland, were beginning to question this rosy, self-congratulatory attitude. Increasingly, much more critical views of the British Empire were being heard.

The Enquiry

In this enquiry you will examine how British attitudes to the Empire were changing in the years after 1900. First of all, you will find out about attitudes towards the Empire at the beginning of the twentieth century, how these changed after the Boer War and how the government responded. Then you will focus on two case studies of India and Ireland to explore changing attitudes in more depth.

Your challenge is to plan a new exhibition, 'Changing attitudes towards Empire'.

The exhibition will be in three parts:

1. Growing doubts and government responses
2. Ruling India
3. Troubles in Ireland

For each part of the exhibition you will:

- Write an introductory panel for visitors to the exhibition.
- Select a picture to be the 'lead image' and provide visitors with the context for this.

Changing attitudes to Empire

This is a portrait of one of the most popular writers in Edwardian Britain – Rudyard Kipling. You have probably seen one of the film versions of his children's story, *The Jungle Book*. Kipling was an Anglo-Indian. He was born in Bombay (now Mumbai) in 1865, but was sent away to school in England at the tender age of five. He hated it and returned to India, to Lahore, aged sixteen. He worked as a journalist, but soon became well known for his short stories, novels and poems.

This is the first verse from a poem about British Empire which Kipling wrote in 1899:

Take up the White Man's burden –
Send forth the best ye breed –
Go bind your sons to exile
To serve your captives' need;
To wait in heavy harness,
On fluttered folk and wild –
Your new-caught, sullen peoples,
Half-devil and half-child.

▶ A portrait of Rudyard Kipling by the artist John Collier, 1891

Kipling had a complex view of the British Empire. He saw running the Empire as a 'burden' – a duty to serve the people of the Empire, whom he admits have become 'captives', 'new-caught'. Like many people in Britain at the beginning of the twentieth century, Kipling thought that the British Empire was a force for good in the world. This view was reinforced through advertising, newspapers and children's books.

Advertising

Edwardian advertisements often encouraged people to buy goods made or grown in the British Empire. They also used images of the Empire to sell products made in Britain.

Reflect

How did this advertisement help to create a positive attitude towards the British Empire?

The first step towards lightening

The White Man's Burden

is through teaching the virtues of cleanliness.

Pears' Soap

is a potent factor in brightening the dark corners of the earth as civilization advances, while amongst the cultured of all nations it holds the highest place—it is the ideal toilet soap.

Newspapers

From 1870 every child had to go to school and the resulting rise in literacy opened the way to new mass-circulation newspapers. One of these was the *Daily Mail*, launched in 1896 and costing ½ penny, half the price of other newspapers. Its owners, Alfred and Harold Harmsworth, were great supporters of the Empire and used the newspaper to publish articles praising '*The champion of the greatness, the superiority of the Empire*'.

Reflect

Why were newspapers more important for shaping people's attitudes in Edwardian Britain than they are today?

◀ A man in Shropshire reading the *Daily Mail*. In the early years of the twentieth century the *Daily Mail* became a popular newspaper with working class people, as this posed photograph shows

Children's books

It was hard for children to avoid the Empire at school, especially public schools, which set out to train boys to run distant parts of the Empire. Maps of the Empire, like the one on page 63, were hung on the classroom walls. History lessons were filled with stories of Empire-building heroes, such as Wolfe of Canada, and Clive of India. Out of school, Edwardian children loved to read adventure stories, by writers like Rider Haggard, Jack London and G. A. Henty. These authors wrote of exciting British deeds in distant countries.

Reflect

Why do you think story books like the one here were so popular with Edwardian children?

▶ A children's story book by G. A. Henty, 1896

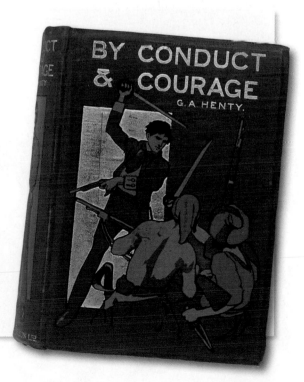

▲ A children's story book by G. A. Henty, 1896

The impact of the Boer War

There had been doubts before about some of the things the British had done to achieve the rapid expansion of their Empire, but it was the Boer War of 1899–1902 which caused a real division in attitudes.

The Boers were South Africans of Dutch origin, mainly farmers (*boer* = farmer). They lived in two independent republics, Transvaal and the Orange Free State, north of the British possessions in Cape Colony and Natal. British imperialists in southern Africa, like Cecil Rhodes, saw the Boers as a block on British expansion northwards up the east side of Africa. This would allow Cape Colony to link up with other British colonies such as Rhodesia, which was named after Rhodes.

▶ A map of southern Africa in 1900

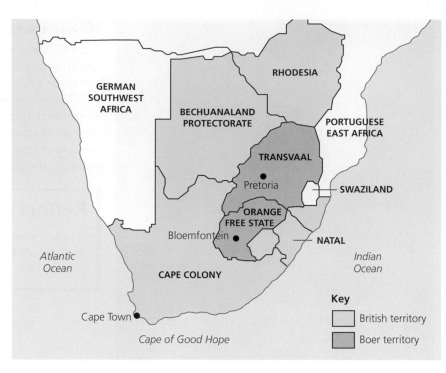

Conflict

When war broke out in October 1899 the British expected an easy victory. However, the Boers knew the territory, were used to handling guns and were brilliantly led. By the end of 1899 they had besieged the British in Ladysmith, Mafeking and Kimberley and inflicted three defeats in 'Black Week', December 1899. Nearly 3000 British soldiers were killed. The British were forced to pour in more troops and by the end of 1900 were in control of most of Boer territory. However, the Boers would not accept defeat and turned to guerrilla tactics.

The British response was to deprive the Boers of their bases with a clearance programme. Across the whole of the Boer republics, 8000 blockhouses were built every 1½ miles and thousands of soldiers moved slowly across the land, burning their farmhouses, poisoning wells and pouring salt on the fields. In total, around 30,000 Boer farms were destroyed. Now homeless, Boer families were put in what the British named 'concentration camps'. Conditions in the camps were appalling. When people in Britain read about what was happening, many were shocked. Attitudes towards the British Empire began to change.

◀ A painting of a burning Boer farm by R. Caton Woodville, 1901

Emily Hobhouse

News of the concentration camps in South Africa was brought to Britain by Emily Hobhouse. She came from a radical Liberal family and was firmly opposed to the Boer War. When she heard about the concentration camps she decided to visit South Africa and see for herself. She reported:

◄ Emily Hobhouse

> When the eight, ten or twelve people who lived in the bell tent were squeezed into it to find shelter against the heat of the sun, the dust or the rain, there was no room to stir and the air in the tent was beyond description, even though the flaps were rolled up properly and fastened. Soap was an article that was not dispensed. The water supply was inadequate. No bedstead or mattress was procurable. Fuel was scarce and had to be collected from the green bushes on the slopes of the kopjes by the people themselves. The rations were extremely meagre and when, as I frequently experienced, the actual quantity dispensed fell short of the amount prescribed, it simply meant famine.

In the famine which Emily Hobhouse reported, 28,000 Boers died, most of them children. When her reports were ignored by MPs in Parliament, she wrote, '*No barbarity in South Africa was as severe as the bleak cruelty of an apathetic parliament*'.

Changing attitudes

The Boer War had cost Britain £250,000 and 45,000 lives. The Liberals who had opposed it in the 1900 election had been condemned in the press as 'pro-Boer'. As news of what was happening in South Africa became known, public opinion changed. In 1901 Lloyd George called it '*A war of extermination ... the savagery of which will stain the name of this country.*' He was right – Britain was criticised around the world. The Boer War helped to sweep them to election victory in 1906.

A major critic of the British Empire at the time was the economist J. A. Hobson. His criticism was based on two main points:

1. **Running the Empire was a huge expense for the British people.**
   This Empire had to be governed and, in some cases, defended. The Indian Army, for example, consisted of 74,000 British and 157,000 Indians. All these government officials and soldiers cost money, paid for by the British taxpayer.
2. **Only a few people benefited from the Empire.** Imperialism resulted in a few people becoming very rich and a mass remaining very poor. The rich needed to find outlets for their capital beyond Britain, and the Empire provided it. £230 million flowed into Britain every year from imperial investments – into the hands of a few investors. They were not only rich, but powerful, directing British foreign policy into wars for profit – like the Boer War, called by some '*a squalid capitalist war to protect Rhodes' investments.*' As for the peoples over whom the British ruled, Hobson argued that there was little real benefit to them either.

In the early years of the twentieth century, a rather different attitude towards the Empire began to be heard: not talk of glory, but of responsibility. Having acquired so many lands, many people began to argue that the British had a duty to improve them by developing agriculture, transport and commerce. Ruling over so many people, it was Britain's responsibility to provide education and justice and to begin to involve them in government – even, at some point in the future, to allow them to govern themselves.

The Government argues back

Supporters of Empire were aware that it was coming under serious criticism. They also knew that for many British people, the Empire meant nothing much at all. So, in the years after 1903, the government began a deliberate campaign to promote positive images of the Empire.

Empire Day

From 1904, schools and whole communities were encouraged to hold 'Empire Day' celebrations on 24 May each year. They were aimed mainly at children, to remind them that *'... they formed part of the British Empire, and that they might think with others in lands across the sea, what it meant to be sons and daughters of such a glorious Empire.'*

On Empire Day children were let off school early. They saluted the Union Jack, listened to speeches of the virtues and benefits of the Empire, and to stories of its heroes. There was often a pageant, usually involving a figure dressed as 'Britannia', to symbolise Britain, with others dressed up to represent people from different parts of the Empire. In some places, bonfires and fireworks brought the day to an end.

But not everyone thought that Empire Day was a good idea. Labour councils such as that in Battersea in London refused to take part in Empire Day, as they saw it as imperial propaganda.

▼ A photograph of Empire Day in Clerkenwell, c. 1910

Colonial Office photographs

In 1907 the Colonial Office in London decided to tackle the apathy that many British people felt about the Empire. They appointed an official photographer and sent him to travel round the Empire for three years, with a brief to take photographs of *'the native characteristics of the country and the super-added characteristics due to British rule'*. The Colonial Office selected photographs to turn into 'lantern slides' (an early form of image projection) which were shown in towns and villages all over Britain. Below you can see three of the photographs from India.

Reflect

What impressions of India at the beginning of the twentieth century were these photographs trying to give?

◀ Snake charmers at Benares

▶ A view of the Lansdownne Bridge over the river Indus

◀ A gymnastics class at the Government High School, Peshwar

Record

Plan the first part of the new exhibition: 'Changing attitudes towards Empire'.

This should summarise:

- Positive attitudes towards the British Empire in 1900
- How the Boer War changed attitudes
- How the government responded

- Write an introductory panel for visitors to the exhibition which covers these three things.
- Select one picture to be the 'lead image' for this part of the exhibition. This could be a picture from pages 62–69 or one you have found in an image search. Write a short piece of text to provide visitors with the information they need to understand the image.

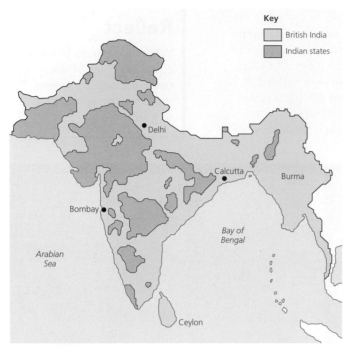

Key
British India
Indian states

▲ British India in 1900. It included the present states of India, Pakistan, Bangladesh, Sri Lanka and Burma

Delhi

Calcutta

Burma

Bombay

Bay of Bengal

Arabian Sea

Ceylon

▼ Lord Curzon with the Nizam of Hyderabad, 1902. As an aristocrat himself. Curzon felt at home with the native princes

Ruling India

As a result of the piece-by-piece way in which the British took over South East Asia, British India (or 'The Raj' as it was often called) was a jumble of different states and provinces. About 60 per cent of the territory (shaded green on this map) was ruled directly by the British. The other 40 per cent was, in theory, ruled by Indian princes (maharajas). In reality, the princes owed loyalty to the British Crown and had a British 'Resident' to 'advise' them. Over them all was the Viceroy, the representative of the British monarch and ruler of 300 million people. In this section you will discover how three different Viceroys represented changing attitudes towards the Raj.

Lord Curzon, 1899–1905

The Viceroy from 1899 to 1905 was Lord Curzon, an English aristocrat, with his own stately home in Derbyshire. He was a convinced imperialist. The British Empire was, he believed: *'the greatest instrument for good that the world has ever seen'*.

Curzon believed that aristocrats, like himself, made the best rulers. He spent a lot of time with the Indian princes and encouraged them to be loyal to the British Empire. At the same time, he made sure that they had no real power. Curzon founded the Imperial Cadet Corps to give Indian princes and aristocrats military training, but he did not allow them to command any troops.

The Delhi Durbar, 1903

Curzon relished the opportunity to organise a Coronation Durbar. This ceremony to celebrate the coronation of the new king, Edward VII, took place in Delhi over the New Year, 1902–3. Curzon was determined to make the Durbar the greatest spectacle India had ever seen. He also ensured that it expressed very clearly his attitude towards the maharajas and to British rule in India.

The Durbar was an enormous undertaking. A city of tents was created on the outskirts of Delhi to accommodate the large number of guests. The encampment had its own railway, shops and police, and water and electricity supply. The ten-day Delhi Durbar included exhibitions of Indian arts and crafts, sports, military reviews, polo matches, banquets and dances. The main event was a huge procession. Maharajas were requested to wear their largest jewels and each took part in the procession on their own highly decorated elephant. The lead elephant carried Lord and Lady Curzon. The 1903 Durbar demonstrated very clearly that the British were in charge.

▲ Lord and Lady Curzon on their elephant at the Delhi Durbar of 1903

Curzon's rule

> # Reflect
>
> What do the following decisions made by Curzon tell us about his attitudes to the British Empire in India?

► Lord Curzon in the robes of the Viceroy of India, 1899

- Curzon had a deep interest in Indian history and culture. He had the Taj Mahal restored when it was in danger of becoming a ruin. He sent teams of archaeologists and architects to restore other important Indian buildings.
- In 1902 Curzon was outraged when some members of the cavalry regiment, the 9th Lancers, brutally attacked an Indian and left him dying outside their camp. The 9th Lancers could not discover the culprits so Curzon punished the whole regiment by cancelling all leave for nine months.
- There were an increasing number of educated Indians, often with degrees from Indian or British universities. Curzon thought that these men were inferior and called them 'Bengali babus'. They were not allowed to apply for senior posts in the Indian Civil Service. Not one Indian was allowed to become a member of the Viceroy's Executive Council.
- In 1899–1900 there was a major famine in India and over 6 million people died. Curzon was criticised for doing little to help the famine victims. In his view, too much money spent on famine relief would have undermined India's economy.
- The Province of Bengal was a mixture of ancient Indian states containing 85 million people. For years, the Indian Civil Service had found it difficult to administer Bengal efficiently. In 1905, without consulting any of its inhabitants, Curzon decided to partition Bengal. This created enormous problems and there was much opposition to Curzon's decision.

▲ Lord Minto c. 1906

▲ John Morley, 1890

Lord Minto, 1905–10

Curzon's successor was Lord Minto. He faced some immediate challenges particularly from the Indian nationalists who wanted to end British rule in India. Curzon's partition of Bengal had led to unrest among nationalists. Some young men had organised themselves into small and well-disciplined groups and had begun to use bombs to kill British people in India. Minto had been a soldier and was determined to crush the violence and unrest. However, he had to work with the new Liberal government in Britain which had a very different attitude from the Conservatives.

The Morley-Minto Reforms

The Liberal Secretary of State for India, John Morley, was a radical and anti-imperialist who had opposed the Boer War. In India he was in favour of reform to give Indian people a greater role in ruling their country. He wrote to Minto: '*Reforms may not save the Raj, but if they don't, nothing else will*'.

Minto replied: '*I am afraid I must utterly disagree. The Raj will not disappear in India as long as the British race remains what it is, because we shall fight for the Raj as hard as we have ever fought ... and we shall win.*'

Out of these two very differing attitudes came a two-pronged policy:

1. Violent opposition was crushed by deporting nationalist leaders and putting the press under strict censorship.
2. Concessions were made towards more Indian participation in government through the 'Morley–Minto Reforms' of 1909. For the first time there were elections to the provincial legislative councils, whose members had previously been simply appointed by the British. An Indian was chosen by the British to join the Viceroy's Executive Council. To protect the Muslim minority there was a separate electorate for Muslims. These reforms did not go nearly far enough for nationalists in the Indian National Congress, but it was a step towards democracy.

Reflect

How would you sum up the changing British attitudes to imperial rule in India, 1905–10?

Lord Hardinge, 1910–16

The next Viceroy, Lord Hardinge, was a diplomat, without Curzon's air of superiority. Despite an assassination attempt on Hardinge in 1912, relations between the British and Indian nationalists improved.

Hardinge supported the Morley–Minto Reforms. He reversed Curzon's unpopular decision to split Bengal. He also supported Indian opposition to the increasingly racist policies of the South African government, where many Indians lived and worked. In 1915 one of them, Mohandas Gandhi, returned to India and was soon a key figure in the Indian Nation Congress, preaching a doctrine of non-violent protest. Hardinge expressed his admiration for Gandhi.

The Delhi Durbar, 1910

The accession to the throne in 1910 of a new king, George V, gave Hardinge the opportunity to hold another Coronation Durbar in December 1911. There was the same tent city outside Delhi, the same massed lines of troops and the same gathering of princes to pay homage to their British overlord. But there were differences, revealing a change in attitude. This time the new king came in person. George V had already visited India before he was king, during Curzon's viceroyalty and had not been impressed. He had written critically in his diary about British attitude towards the Indians: 'We are too much inclined to look upon them as a conquered and down-trodden race, and the Native, who is becoming more and more educated, realises this.'

At the Durbar of 1910 the maharajas once again appeared in their finery, but this time the Indians were seated much closer to the king and queen. In addition to the Durbar itself, the king also held a 'darshan', a much more informal appearance on a balcony, to which half a million people came.

At the Durbar the king made a surprise announcement that the capital would be transferred from Calcutta (now Kolkata) to Delhi. This was hugely popular in Delhi and wrong-footed the Indian nationalists in Calcutta. Hardinge's efforts to improve relations with the Indian people paid off in the First World War when many Indian soldiers fought for Britain.

▲ Lord Hardinge c. 1905

▼ The 'darshan' of George V, 1910

Record

Plan the second part of the new exhibition: 'Changing attitudes towards Empire'.

● Write an introductory panel for visitors which summarises the changing attitudes to British rule in India in the period 1900–16.

● Select one picture to be the 'lead image' for this part of the exhibition. This could be a picture from pages 70–73 or one you have found through an image search. Write a short piece of text to provide visitors with the information they need to understand the image.

Crisis in Ireland

To many British people in 1900, Ireland seemed to be just a part of Britain, like Wales and Scotland, not an imperial possession. By the Irish Act of Union of 1800, Ireland was represented in Parliament by 100 MPs and 28 peers. But Irish Nationalism had grown strongly through the nineteenth century. Nationalists pointed out that, like other parts of the British Empire, Ireland was a conquered land, taken by the English.

Following the seventeenth-century conquest, the Irish were dispossessed of their land, which went to English and Scottish settlers. Most importantly, the majority of the population had remained Roman Catholic, unaffected by the Protestant Reformation in mainland Britain. The exception to this was the north east of Ireland, the province of Ulster, where a large influx of British settlers meant that Protestants were in a majority. Ulster had become the most industrialised part of Ireland, centred round the great shipbuilding and manufacturing city of Belfast. The people of Ulster saw themselves as part of Britain, sharing their religion and way of life, quite different from the mainly rural, small-farming, Roman Catholic rest of Ireland. They called themselves Unionists, wanting to preserve the Union with Britain. The Unionists had widespread support in England, especially from imperialists and Conservatives.

Nineteenth-century Irish nationalism had taken both violent and legal approaches. While the Fenians exploded bombs in London and assassinated English officials, the Irish National Party worked through Parliament. They pressed Parliament to vote for Home Rule, but the Home Rule bills of 1886 and 1893 were both defeated.

Crisis, 1910–14

After 1910 the question of Home Rule for Ireland took a dramatic turn. In the elections of 1910 the Liberals lost their majority and there was a hung Parliament. The Liberals were now dependent on Irish Nationalist support. This greatly increased the influence of the Nationalists. They helped the Liberals get through their great welfare reforms and the Parliament Act, weakening the House of Lords (see page 37).

Then came their payback time. The Liberals introduced a Home Rule bill in 1912, setting up an Irish Parliament in Dublin with powers over all internal Irish affairs, but with Ireland still part of the Empire. This was highly alarming to the people of Ulster and this map of the election results of 1910 shows why. The Unionists saw themselves becoming a minority in a country with a different economy and different religious beliefs.

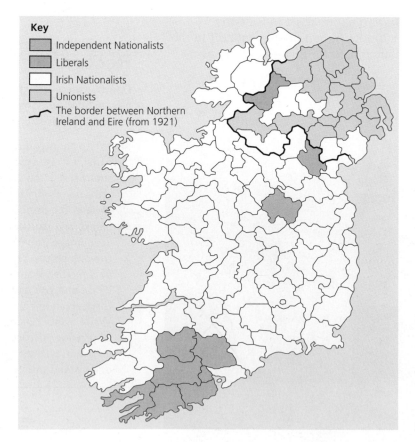

◄ The election results of 1910

In January 1913 an Ulster Volunteer Force (UVF) was formed and soon had 40,000 members. In April 1914, 25,000 rifles and 3½ million rounds of ammunition were successfully smuggled through the port of Larne. This was a very well-organised operation, with convoys of motor cars arriving at the port by night and taking away consignments of weapons to be hidden until they might be needed. This armed Ulster resistance was undoubtedly illegal, but had considerable support in England, from the Conservative Party and even the king.

▲ Sir Edward Carson, Unionist leader, reviewing some of the UVF with their weapons, 1914

Meanwhile in the rest of Ireland, Nationalists were angered by the events in Ulster, and by the apparent support the Unionists were getting. In 1913 a Nationalist force was raised, called the Irish Volunteers. By 1914 they outnumbered the UVF, although they were not as well armed. Soon, the Irish Republican Brotherhood, or Fenians, were in control of the Volunteers. The Fenians were committed to an armed struggle for complete independence. They rejected the terms of the Home Rule Act, which left Ireland still part of the Empire, under the British crown, with many decisions still taken in London.

It seemed that civil war was likely to break out in Ireland at any moment. Home Rule for Ireland became law in September 1914, but by then Britain was at war and the process was suspended. The much greater violence of the World War meant that violence in Ireland was avoided ... for the time being.

Reflect

In your view, how far were British attitudes to blame for the crisis in 1914?

▼ A company of National Volunteers from Boyle, County Roscommon drilling at Keash, County Sligo, in 1914

The Easter Rising

Around 150,000 Irishmen fought in the British Army during the war. Both Protestants from Ulster and Catholics from the south took part in the battle of the Somme, suffering serious casualties. The leader of the Irish Nationalist MPs, John Redmond, was keen to show the British government that his brand of moderate nationalism embraced loyalty to Britain and personally encouraged Irishmen to join up. He made recruiting speeches and appeared on posters.

▲ A First World War Recruitment Poster produced by the Irish Nationalist Party

Easter Monday, 1916

But while some Irishmen were fighting for Britain on the Western Front, others were preparing an armed rebellion against British rule. The rebels believed that their action would revive Irish nationalism before it was lost in the common struggle with Germany.

In the end just 1600 armed rebels took up positions at various places around Dublin on Easter Monday, 1916. At their headquarters in the General Post Office in O'Connell Street, the main shopping street, they declared themselves the Provisional Government of an independent Irish Republic.

The poet Padraig Pearse read their proclamation:

> IRISHMEN AND IRISHWOMEN: In the name of God and of the dead generations from which she receives her old tradition of nationhood, Ireland, through us, summons her children to her flag and strikes for her freedom.

At first the British were taken by surprise and suffered some casualties. However, reinforcements were called up, including heavy machine guns, artillery and a gunship, the *Helga*. The rebels came under heavy shelling and they surrendered after six days when the Post Office was gutted by fire.

A total of 132 soldiers and police were killed, along with 49 rebels. Over 250 civilians were killed and 2200 wounded in the shooting. Several buildings in the centre of Dublin lay in ruins.

Many people in Dublin reacted to the Rising with fury and disgust. Arrested rebels were abused and pelted with tomatoes as they were marched to prison. But the heavy-handed British reaction completely changed the situation. Asquith had given the British Commander, General Maxwell, a free hand under martial law to crush the Rising and its supporters. Maxwell had 3500 possible sympathisers arrested, many of whom had been nowhere near Dublin. Some were tried in a military court, and sent to prison in England. Within a week of the end of the Rising, the fifteen leaders were shot by firing squad. This included James Connolly, dying from his wounds, who was carried out to the prison yard on a stretcher, tied to a chair and shot.

The Irish people were outraged. Popular support swung away from Redmond and his party's policy of moderation and working with the British government. In the first elections after the war, in 1918, *Sinn Fein* ('We ourselves') stood as the party of Irish independence. They won 73 out of the 105 Irish seats and refused to go to London to take them. Instead they met in Dublin and proclaimed themselves the '*Dail Eireann*', the Parliament of Ireland. This was followed by three more years of bloody fighting, until the independent Irish Free State was set up in 1922.

▲ The post office (right) and other buildings in the centre of Dublin after the Easter Rising

Record

Plan the final part of the new exhibition: 'Changing attitudes towards Empire'.

● Write an introductory panel for visitors which summarises changing British attitudes towards Ireland after 1910. You might find it helpful to present the panel as an annotated timeline.

● Select one picture to be the 'lead image' for this part of the exhibition. This could be a picture from pages 74–77 or one you have found through an image search. Write a short piece of text to provide visitors with the information they need to understand the image.

Review

Decide on an overall title for the exhibition.

Different historians' interpretations of the British Empire

As you have discovered, people in Edwardian Britain had very different attitudes towards the Empire. In more recent times, historians continue to disagree about the British Empire. Some argue that the Empire, which ruled so much of the world in the period 1900–18, was a force for good. Others feel strongly that the British Empire did little to help colonised people and that it could often be a brutal force which did great harm.

In 2001 the *BBC History Magazine* asked two respected historians, Denis Judd and Lawrence James, whether the British Empire was a force for good or a force for bad. Here are summaries of what they said.

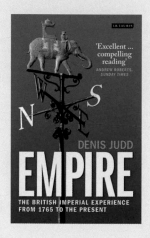

The British Empire was a force for bad in the world

When imperialists boasted that '*the sun never set on the British Empire*', critics said that this was because God didn't trust the British in the dark. Much of what the British got up to in their Empire was selfish and destructive.

Imperialists pretended that imperial rule was based on the consent of the colonised people, but the British Empire could never be based on consent. Colonised people were given no say in the running of the colonies. Territories were annexed to serve British needs, not to improve the lives of colonised people. The British often created divisions between people in their colonies. It is not surprising that in many colonies tribal and ethnic conflict followed independence.

Imperial rule damaged the economies of different colonies. Before colonisation many territories were self-sufficient in food. Under British rule colonies were often dependent on one cash crop such as rubber, sugar and coffee. After independence a sharp fall in the price of one of these crops could result in poverty and hunger for millions of people.

Perhaps the worst damage was to the self-esteem of the colonised people. The British treated the people they ruled like children. To be ruled by a people from a distant land who often tried to destroy aspects of your culture was a humiliating experience.

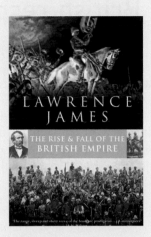

The British Empire was a force for good in the world

At first the Empire was about making money, but during the nineteenth and twentieth centuries the British improved the lives of millions of people. The Empire was governed for the benefit of its subjects. The Empire was never perfect, but the colonial rulers were honest and dedicated men who were often respected by colonised people. The British Empire was run according to the rule of law. Colonial officials could not do as they wished, but had to answer to Parliament in London.

The British Empire took science and technology to many different parts of the world. British-built railways, bridges and canals improved communications in many territories. Hospitals and medical centres led to better health care.

Important cultural changes took place in British colonies. Colonised people were educated in British schools and attended Christian churches. English was widely spoken throughout the Empire and this means that former British colonies are in a strong position to trade and prosper in the modern world.

Reflect

Exactly how do these two interpretations of the British Empire differ? What might explain the differences between them?

Total war

How did the British respond, 1914–18?

In August 1914 Britain went to war in northern Europe. Just a few months later, the war came to Britain.

Early in the morning of 16 December, people were beginning to go about their lives in the shipbuilding town of Hartlepool in north east England when three large grey German battle cruisers appeared out at sea. What happened next was recalled 50 years later by Harry Bell, then fourteen years old, and already at work:

I was working at Gray's Central Shipyard. I had just finished warming my can of tea at about 8.20 a.m. when gunfire could be heard and everybody went outside to see what was happening. In a few seconds a shell hit the office and blew nearly all of it into the air and at the same time railway wagons were being blown sky-high. Men who were running in that direction turned and made their way towards the back gate leading to Slag Island Quay. Nearing this gate I climbed on one of the uprights and saw that the gasometers were on fire …

Reaching the corner of Middleton Road and Hartlepool Road I noticed a young boy stretched over the tramlines face downwards and when I went over to him I saw that he was dead with nearly all his chest blown away. A few yards further on I saw Barney Hodgson pinned against the church wall and bleeding very badly. I ran towards him and he said 'Keep running, son, I'm done for'.

When I reached home my mother was propped up against the wall of our house with blood running from her like water from a tap and in the road opposite was a boy by the name of Joseph Jacobs, who was dead. I ran to the bottom of our street and took a barrow from the yard and ran back with it to our house to put my mother on it to take her to hospital. It was then that my brother Tom came up and between us we got my mother and the boy Jacobs on to the cart. Later we stopped a coal cart and asked the driver to take them to hospital, which he did.

At the mortuary I identified our youngest brother who had been killed. Another brother was in hospital with leg injuries. Our family's total casualties were my mother – a lost leg and multiple injuries, a brother killed, a brother with leg injuries and a nephew killed.

▼ A house in Hartlepool after the German bombardment in December 1914

The nature of total war

The war that started on 4 August 1914 was soon being called 'total war'. As we have just seen, one way in which this war was different was that civilians in their homes were killed by enemy action. What else did total war mean?

- The numbers of fighting men on each side, and the weapons they used, placed huge demands on the resources of the nations involved. A modern industrialised state like Britain could only hope to win the war by producing more weapons than the enemy.
- The British government calculated that every fighting man needed three others working to support him. This involved every man and, eventually, every woman in the country: another side to total war.
- Although everyone hoped in August 1914 that the war would be 'over by Christmas', it eventually lasted more than four years, until November 1918. It took time for the government to realise what this meant, and its response changed radically as the war went on.

Reflect

Which of these aspects of 'total war' do you think people in Britain would have found most challenging?

An outline of Britain's war, 1914–18

1914	4 August: Britain declares war on Germany.
	5 August: Government calls for 100,000 volunteers to join the army.
	8 August: Defence of the Realm Act (DORA) gives the government extra powers.
1915	May: Serious shortage of ammunition weakens the British Army.
1916	2 March: Conscription of troops into Britain's army begins.
	7 December: Lloyd George becomes Prime Minster.
1917	January: German submarine successes cause food shortages in Britain.
1918	January: The demands of war drag on into a fourth year.
	11 November: Armistice – war ends.

The Enquiry

Your challenge in this enquiry is to find out how the government and the people responded to the demands of this 'total war'. It was a new type of war so it made new demands and created new types of response. It also lasted far longer than most people had expected and this meant that both the demands and the responses changed over time.

In this enquiry you will learn about:

- Government responses to the demands of the war
- Men's responses to the demands of war
- Women's responses to the demands of war.

As you work through the enquiry you will make a set of 'response cards'. Each one will identify a way in which the government or the people responded to the war.

On one side of the card you will note down the date and briefly summarise the response. On the other side of the card you will explain why that response happened at that particular time.

At the end of the enquiry, you will use your cards to help you to decide how well you think Britain met the demands of war overall.

Government responses to the changing demands of war

Record

As you read pages 82–87, make your first few 'response cards' as explained on page 81.

Recruiting volunteers

British governments had always prioritised the navy over the army. The job of the navy was to protect the island of Britain, its sea-going trade and its Empire. In the 1914 budget the Navy received £51 million and the Army £29 million. As a result, the British Army in 1914 was small – about a quarter of a million men, largely scattered across the British Empire as a sort of police force, with another half a million in reserve. When the Kaiser called it 'a contemptibly little army' he was comparing it with the German army, which had 3.8 million men under arms within a week of the outbreak of war in August 1914.

In a mood of optimistic patriotism, people talked of the war being 'over by Christmas'. The government, however, was more realistic. Kitchener, the old war hero brought into the Cabinet, realised that Britain was going to need a mass army if it was to take part in the land war in Europe. He called at once for 100,000 volunteers; within eight weeks 750,000 had volunteered. In September there was a call for another 500,000 and the age limit was raised to 35 with a special appeal to married men.

Reflect

How do the decorations on this recruitment tram encourage men to join the Army?

▼ A recruitment tram. Speakers often toured cities by tram, encouraging men to join the army. This one is from Leeds

Propaganda

In August 1914, Lloyd George was given the job of setting up the War Propaganda Bureau (WPB). Advertising was already an important industry and the skills of artists and copywriters were put to use by the WPB. The WPB produced some anti-German propaganda, such as when it publicised horror stories of atrocities in Belgium. But its main task was to encourage recruitment for the volunteer army. A total of 12.5 million recruiting posters were produced, in over 160 different designs.

One of the most famous posters of all time was the one shown here (right), designed to catch the attention of any young man wherever he looked. The figure pointing out at the viewer is Lord Kitchener.

Other recruitment posters, such as those below, drew on the idea of total war to encourage men to join the Army or Navy. In one (below right), a young boy scout is shown handing a package from home to a soldier serving overseas. Part of the propaganda campaign encouraged children to make or collect things that would make life more comfortable for the troops. In this way they too would feel part of the war effort.

Reflect

What event from December 1914 does the poster below left refer to?

How do the two posters below each draw on the idea of 'total war' to achieve their effect?

▲▼ British propaganda posters from 1914–1915

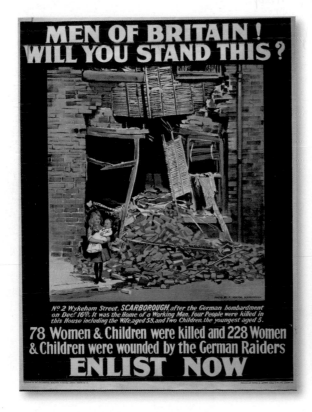

Conscription

By late 1915 the British Army numbered 2 million men. However, as the graph below shows, the early flood of volunteers had dropped greatly, and numbers were often below the government's target. Creating an army of volunteers had also brought some problems, as there was nothing to stop workers in key industries from joining up. One-fifth of all miners and a quarter of all chemical and explosives workers, for example, had 'answered their country's call'. The number of casualties continued to grow and the war showed no sign of ending. The need to introduce conscription was becoming unanswerable.

The Liberals' concerns

Conscripting people into the Army or Navy would mean that the government would be requiring British citizens to lay their lives on the line, to fight and perhaps die for the state. This was a huge step to take. The Liberal government had always resisted conscription as it ran against some of their fundamental principles: the right of citizens to be in control of their own lives, the belief that government should play as little a part as possible in their lives.

The Military Service Act

Conscription was eventually introduced in March 1916 after the passing of the Military Service Act in January. At first single men aged between 19 and 41 could be called up; this was extended to married men in May 1916. Men doing jobs considered important for the war effort, called 'restricted occupations', were exempted. By the end of the war, 4 million men had been conscripted.

THE
MILITARY SERVICE ACT,
1916,

APPLIES TO UNMARRIED MEN WHO, ON AUGUST 15th, 1915, WERE 18 YEARS OF AGE OR OVER AND WHO WILL NOT BE 41 YEARS OF AGE ON MARCH 2nd, 1916.

ALL MEN (NOT EXCEPTED OR EXEMPTED),

between the above ages who, on November 2nd, 1915, were Unmarried or Widowers without any Child dependent on them will, on

Thursday, March 2nd, 1916

BE DEEMED TO BE ENLISTED FOR THE PERIOD OF THE WAR.

They will be placed in the Reserve until Called Up in their Class.

MEN EXCEPTED:

SOLDIERS, including Territorials who have volunteered for Foreign Service;
MEN serving in the NAVY or ROYAL MARINES;
MEN DISCHARGED from ARMY or NAVY, disabled or ill, or TIME-EXPIRED MEN;
MEN REJECTED for the ARMY since AUGUST 14th, 1915;
CLERGYMEN, PRIESTS, and MINISTERS OF RELIGION;
VISITORS from the DOMINIONS.

MEN WHO MAY BE EXEMPTED BY LOCAL TRIBUNALS:

Men more useful to the Nation in their present employments;
Men in whose case Military Service would cause serious hardship owing to exceptional financial or business obligations or domestic position;
Men who are ill or infirm;
Men who conscientiously object to combatant service. If the Tribunal thinks fit, men may, on this ground, be (a) exempted from combatant service only (not non-combatant service), or (b) exempted on condition that they are engaged in work of National importance.

Up to March 2nd, a man can apply to his Local Tribunal for a certificate of exemption. There is a Right of Appeal. He will not be called up until his case has been dealt with finally.
Certificates of exemption may be absolute, conditional or temporary. Such certificates can be renewed, varied or withdrawn.
Men retain their Civil Rights until called up and are amenable to Civil Courts only.

DO NOT WAIT UNTIL MARCH 2nd.
ENLIST VOLUNTARILY NOW.

For fuller particulars of the Act, please apply for Leaflet No. 64 to the nearest Post Office, Police Station, or Recruiting Office.

▲ Parliamentary Recruitment Committee poster from 1916

Reflect

Men would have to join the Army or Navy on 2 March. Why do you think this poster urges them to join up before then?

▼ Rates of recruitment to the British armed services, per month 1914–18

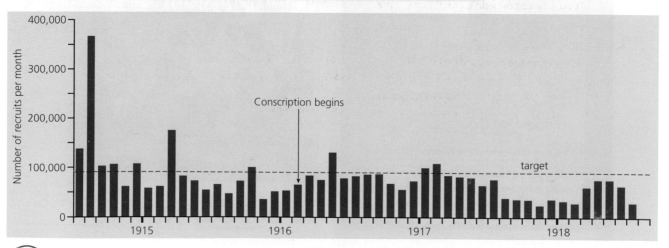

DORA: the government's special powers

'DORA' was the nickname of the <u>D</u>efence <u>o</u>f the <u>R</u>ealm <u>A</u>ct, which was passed on 8 August 1914, just four days into the war. It gave the government some extraordinary and wide-ranging powers, changing the everyday lives of the British people in several ways. We still live with some of DORA's provisions today.

The most far-reaching powers DORA gave the government were the powers to take over any factory, workshop or land. This meant that they could effectively direct the entire economy and was extraordinary for a Liberal government previously committed to keeping the influence of government small. These powers were not used until later in the war, but by the end, the government was in control of munitions factories, coal mines, railways, merchant shipping and agricultural production, indirectly employing a total of 3 million workers. We will find out how this happened and the impact it made on the next page.

Examples of how the government used DORA

Dealing with spies

The concerns of the government in August 1914 can be seen in some of the other powers DORA gave them. At that time, many believed that Britain was full of German spies. DORA therefore banned activities which might be carried out by those collecting information or helping Zeppelin raiders navigate over Britain:

- Loitering near bridges or tunnels
- Buying binoculars
- Flying kites
- Lighting bonfires
- Ringing church bells
- Using invisible ink

Alcohol

The government was worried about alcoholism among workers weakening the war effort. DORA allowed publicans to water down their beer and banned what was called 'treating' – buying rounds of drinks for others.

Before the war most pubs opened as long as they liked: DORA introduced licensing hours, normally 12.00 to 2.30 p.m. and 6.30 p.m. to 9.30 p.m. These restrictions continued until the 1980s.

Many were encouraged to 'take the pledge' not to drink any alcohol at all until the war was over. King George V did so, and was annoyed that so few senior politicians did the same.

British Summer Time

This was originally called 'Daylight Saving Time' and was introduced in 1916. By 'putting the clocks forward' one hour from April through to September, better use was made of early morning light and energy was saved. This has continued until the present day, except for 'double summer time' in the Second World War.

Secrecy and censorship

Actions which might hinder the British war effort or help the enemy, like talking about the movement of troops or ships, were banned. DORA also gave the government the power of censorship, including the right to open letters and telegrams. If a letter contained any information which the enemy might find useful, the sender might receive a notice like the one below.

Postal Censorship.

The communication returned in this cover constitutes a breach of the Defence of the Realm Regulations. The writer is warned to be more careful in future.

N.B.—The communication will be allowed to proceed if the passage or passages referring to *Zepplein raids etc* are omitted, and if it is re-posted to the addressee in the usual way.

▲ British censorship note, 1916

Newspapers were also censored. DORA was very clear:

> No person shall by word of mouth or in writing spread reports likely to cause disaffection or alarm among any of His Majesty's forces or among the civilian population.

The Army was determined to control the news from the front. Their view was that the public should be told as little as possible. One reporter, Philip Gibbs, visited the Front Line, but was seized, removed and told that if he appeared again he would be shot. It was only after the war that the actual numbers killed at the Battle of the Somme, for example, became public knowledge.

Officers routinely censored the letters home from the trenches by the men under their command, in case they gave useful information to the enemy if they were intercepted or loosely talked about in Britain.

DELIVERING THE GOODS.

▲ A cartoon from *Punch* magazine showing Lloyd George riding to rescue the Army with a cartload of shells, 1915

Wartime production

The war put a strain on the nation's ability to produce all it needed.

Munitions

By May 1915 Britain faced a 'shell shortage'. Continuous firing of heavy guns over a long period had not been planned for. Prime Minister Asquith responded by making David Lloyd George Minister of Munitions.

Lloyd George brought energy and imagination to the job. He hired business leaders to rationalise the whole munitions industry. He ordered the setting up of 73 munitions factories and, while these were being built, he used the powers the Government had under DORA to take over railway workshops. By the end of 1915, their skilled workers were producing up to 5000 shells a week, as well as all kinds of military vehicles.

In December 1916, Lloyd George took over as Prime Minister.

Government takeover of industry

For many years before the war, Liberals insisted that governments should play little or no part in the economy. But after 1914 this was set aside. There was a war to be won and DORA gave the government enormous powers. Once Lloyd George had shown the way with the munitions industry, more and more of the economy came under government control. 'Big Government' arrived, and has continued ever since.

Railways. The jumble of companies that ran Britain's railways was making great profits from the wartime increase in rail traffic. Socialists had long called for nationalisation of the railways – and the rest of British industry. This would mean that the government would take over the companies and run the railways in the national interest. The Liberals stopped short of that: the directors of the railway companies continued to operate the system. They were allowed to make profits, but only at pre-war levels, and they were now answerable to the government. As Lloyd George put it: they were not run *by* the government, but *for* the government.

Coal. Coal was the essential fuel for steam-powered rail and sea transport, as well as much of industry. Strikes in the south Wales coalfield in July 1915 brought rapid government response: the miners' union's demands were met at once and the government took over all coal mines in south Wales. The rest of the mines in Britain were taken over in early 1917.

Land. DORA gave the government the powers to take over land as well. In fact, government intervention in agriculture was more indirect: War Agricultural Committees were set up in every county. They advised farmers on what crops to grow, and how.

Shipping. Government intervention took place gradually. In April 1915, to ensure food supplies, they took over all refrigerated space in ships from Australia and New Zealand, then all coastal shipping. In December 1916 all shipping was put under government control.

Reflect

Is it surprising that the Liberal government put so much of British industry under government control in 1914?

Food shortages and rationing

Britain only produced one-third of its own food – the rest had to be imported. The German navy began unrestricted U-boat warfare in January 1917 and soon 300,000 tonnes of shipping were being sunk each month. There were shortages of sugar, potatoes, bread, tea and coal. With no system of rationing, these shortages brought considerable unrest among the civilian population who had to cope with:

● Long queues at the shops
● Rising prices of key items.

Prices in 1917 were estimated to be 80 per cent higher than in 1914. Wages had also risen, but not by nearly as much. The impact of rising prices on poorer families led to strikes for wage increases. There were food riots in east London in March 1917.

The government was reluctant to introduce rationing as yet another step away from the free market which Liberals held so dear. The Ministry of Food tried persuasion at first. Propaganda posters like this one (right) urged people to limit how much bread they ate so that fewer ships would need to carry the precious wheat from the USA or Canada.

By the end of 1917 Britain was said to have only two months' supply of wheat and four days' supply of sugar. Rationing of bread, meat and sugar was eventually introduced in January 1918. Each family was issued with a ration book that showed how much food they were allowed to buy, including sugar, meat, flour, butter, margarine and milk. The shopkeeper would then cut out the stamps in the book in return for the food provided. Even King George V and Queen Mary had ration books.

Individuals or shopkeepers who broke the rationing rules faced very severe fines as the poster below shows. A fine of £20 was equal to over a year's pay for a soldier serving in the army. Some offenders were even sent to prison.

▲ British propaganda poster, 1917

◀ An official British notice to the public, 1918

DEFENCE OF THE REALM. E.P. 6.

MINISTRY OF FOOD.

BREACHES OF THE RATIONING ORDER

The undermentioned convictions have been recently obtained:–

Court	Date	Nature of Offence	Result
HENDON	29th Aug., 1918	Unlawfully obtaining and using ration books	3 Months' Imprisonment
WEST HAM	29th Aug., 1918	Being a retailer & failing to detach proper number of coupons	Fined £20
SMETHWICK	22nd July, 1918	Obtaining meat in excess quantities	Fined £50 & £5 5s. costs
OLD STREET	4th Sept., 1918	Being a retailer selling to unregistered customer	Fined £72 & £5 5s. costs
OLD STREET	4th Sept., 1918	Not detaching sufficient coupons for meat sold	Fined £25 & £2 2s. costs
CHESTER-LE-STREET	4th Sept., 1918	Being a retailer returning number of registered customers in excess of counterfoils deposited	Fined £50 & £3 3s. costs
HIGH WYCOMBE	7th Sept., 1918	Making false statement on application for and using Ration Books unlawfully	Fined £40 & £6 4s. costs

Enforcement Branch, Local Authorities Division,
MINISTRY OF FOOD.

Reflect

Why do you think the programme of persuasion did not work?

Record

Finish making your first batch of 'response cards' as explained on page 81. These cards should identify and explain responses that you have learned about on pages 82–87.

Men's responses

Record

As you read pages 88–91, make your next batch of 'response cards' as explained on page 81.

In the first wave of enthusiasm for the new war, recruiting offices, like this one in central London, were overwhelmed.

By mid-September 1914, 750,000 men had responded to Kitchener's call for volunteers to increase the size of the British Army. Three-quarters of a million brave and idealistic young men aged between 19 and 30, from all social classes, signed up to fight for 'three years or until the war is concluded'.

▲ Crowds outside a recruitment office, August 1914

The call to fight

The pressure to enlist was everywhere. Along with the posters (see page 83), some landowners encouraged their tenants to join up and allowed their families to live in their tied cottages rent-free. Some women joined the 'White Feather' campaign: they were encouraged to hand a white feather, a mark of cowardice, to any man of military age not in uniform (much to the annoyance of soldiers home on leave in civilian clothes, or men in civilian war work).

Calls to volunteer were made at all kinds of gatherings – from the stages of music halls, for example, or, as here, after a football match:

> **From the *Yorkshire Post*, September, 1914**
>
> Stirring scenes were witnessed at Leeds City football ground last night at the end of the match. The Lord Mayor addressed the crowd of 4000 spectators, calling for recruits. There was a spirited rush across the field and rousing cheers. Up the steps sturdy young fellows came, to receive an armlet with the national colours. When the rush subsided it was found that the number of volunteers was 149. The Lady Mayoress called for another 51. Another dash was made and the quota quickly filled.

Perhaps the most cynical of all recruiters was Horatio Bottomley. He made up to £100 a time (over £10,000 in today's money) giving speeches which worked up his audience to a patriotic frenzy and ended with an appeal for volunteers. He was not above telling complete lies or making statements that he could not possibly justify. In a speech in Bournemouth in September 1915, when British troops were failing to gain ground at the Battle of Loos and suffering enormous casualties, he argued:

> Ladies and gentlemen, I want you to pull yourselves together and keep your peckers up. I want to assure you that within six weeks of to-day we shall have the Huns on the run. We shall drive them out of France, out of Flanders, out of Belgium, across the Rhine, and back into their own territory. There we shall give them a taste of their own medicine. Bear in mind, I speak of that which I know. Tomorrow it will be officially denied, but take it from me that if Bottomley says so, it is so!

▲ Horatio Bottomley speaking in Trafalgar Square, London 1915

Reflect

Why do you think so many men volunteered to fight in the war?

'Pals battalions'

Many young, working-class men joined up out of patriotism. Others, in these early days of the war, simply wanted a change and an adventure with their mates. The army encouraged 'pals' to join up together on the promise that they would serve together.

Here are the 'Accrington Pals' (officially the 11th battalion of the East Lancs Regiment). Accrington is a town in east Lancashire and every man in the battalion came from that town or nearby.

There was a grim side effect of the pals battalions. Having joined up and served together, many of the 'Accrington Pals' died together on the first day of the Battle of the Somme – 1 July 1916. So many dead at the same time was a disaster for the whole town, with grief-stricken families in every street.

▲ The Accrington Pals on a training course, 1916

Physical requirements

As in the Boer War at the start of the century, army recruitment revealed the effects of poverty on the physical state of working-class recruits. As one recalled:

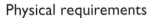

> They asked me my height and I told them. They hummed and haaed about it. I'm five foot six [167 cm] with paper stuffed into my shoes. Anyway, I says to them: 'There's six of my pals joining up, all footballers'. So they says 'Aw, go on let him in'. So I was one of the midgets.

At the beginning of the war, volunteer recruits had to be at least 5ft 6in tall. By May 1915 soldiers only had to be 5ft 3in and the age limit was raised to 40. In July the army agreed to the formation of 'Bantam' battalions, composed of men between 5ft and 5ft 3in in height.

Recruits had to be nineteen years old but many younger men lied their way into the army. Recruiting sergeants often did not check their ages.

Reflect

What was the main attraction of 'pals battalions' for working men?

▼ New British army recruits in France, July 1918

Reflect

How many of the men – or boys – in this photograph of new recruits look nineteen or older?

▲ Lieutenant A.S. Lloyd MC, c. 1914

The response of wealthier men

As you saw on page 80, 70 per cent of the British population were working class, and therefore made up the great majority of recruits. But middle- and upper-class young men also joined up with great enthusiasm. Undergraduates from Oxford and Cambridge Universities volunteered in large numbers, leaving the colleges almost empty and available to be used for officer training. Men of this class felt bound to support the country in which they played such a significant part.

Middle- and upper-class families often had links with the army and most boys had joined the OTC (Officer Training Corps) at their public school and were assured of becoming a junior officer on joining up. An upper- or middle-class young man of nineteen could therefore find himself in charge of a platoon of 30 working-class recruits, some of them old enough to be his father.

This photograph shows just one example, Alan Lloyd, a middle-class young man from Birmingham. On 6 August 1914, he wrote to his fiancée explaining his reasons for joining up:

> This is a life & death struggle with Germany. Everybody who could do something & won't is a beastly unpatriotic kind of person. I … hate flag-wagging & Union Jack hurrahing etc. but I do feel that I might be useful, with my motor or without it, in case of attack by Germany & so I've offered my services

Lloyd was given the rank of second lieutenant as soon as he joined up, and was killed a year later.

Learning to lead

The class system continued into the army. Upper- and middle-class recruits were, on average 5 inches (13 cm) taller than men from the working class. They were expected to buy their own uniforms and received better food.

The trenches threw together men whose lives would have hardly crossed in peacetime. They lived in close proximity and shared the threat of death. It was often a life-changing experience on both sides. Harold MacMillan was Conservative Prime Minster from 1957 to 1963. As a young man he served as an officer on the Western Front and was wounded five times. After education at Eton and Oxford, having to fight alongside ordinary working men affected him deeply. He said later that he:

> learnt for the first time to understand, talk with, and feel at home with a whole class of men.

Junior officers suffered a very high death rate. They were expected to lead their men 'over the top' in attacks on enemy lines and so were prime targets. It has been estimated that the death rate of peers' sons was greater than in the Wars of the Roses in the fifteenth century, and many aristocratic titles died out as a result of the lack of a male heir, killed in this war.

Reflect

Why did such a large proportion of middle- and upper-class men volunteer at the start of the war?

▼ Cambridge University officer training corps, 1914

Conscientious objection

When conscription was reluctantly introduced in March 1916, MPs who opposed it insisted on including the right to refuse to serve on grounds of conscience. Men who exercised this right were Conscientious Objectors (COs). Out of 4 million men who were eventually conscripted there were about 14,000 COs. Three-quarters of them were socialists who said that they had no quarrel with ordinary German workers. They believed that the war was a capitalist war, fought for bosses, bankers, industrialists and kings.

The rest of the COs had religious motives. The Quakers, for example, had a long tradition of Christian pacifism, taking seriously the sixth of the Ten Commandments in the Christian Bible: 'Thou shalt not kill.'

Anyone claiming conscientious objection had to appear before a local tribunal which decided whether their objection was genuine. Many of the tribunals were staffed by army officers who were often biased against conscientious objectors. A member of the tribunal at Shaw, Manchester, told one applicant:

> I think you are exploiting God to save your own skin. A man who would not help to defend his own country and womankind is a coward. You are nothing but a shivering mass of unwholesome fat.

It is not hard to see why people were angry with the COs with so many dying at the Front. Public opinion tended to believe that COs were really just being selfish or cowardly.

▲ Cartoonist's view of a conscientious objector, c. 1916. Its caption reads 'This little pig stayed at home'.

Reflect

What is the cartoon trying to say about conscientious objectors?

How COs were dealt with

Only 400 of the 14,000 COs were given full exemption from the army. About 6000 were let off because they were doing 'work of national importance' and about 5000 accepted the offer of doing non-combatant duties in the army, such as driving ambulances. Around 2600 were rejected completely and told they had to join the army. Half refused, were arrested, sent to an army barracks and told to put on uniform. They would be in serious trouble if they disobeyed an order. Forty were sent to France where they could be shot for disobeying orders in a battle area.

The army soon realised that it could not force someone to change their mind and an uncommitted soldier was no use to them. COs who refused to co-operate were sentenced to prison with hard labour.

After the war, when all other men had earned the right to vote, conscientious objectors were excluded for five years.

▲ The Whiteford brothers of Bristol, photographed c. 1916. Left to right: a fighting soldier, a conscientious objector, an ambulance driver

Reflect

What does this photograph of the Whiteford brothers suggest about men's responses to the First World War?

Record

Finish the 'response cards' that you have been making based on pages 88–91. They should follow the instructions given on page 81.

Women's responses to the war

Record

As you read pages 92–95, make your next batch of 'response cards' as explained on page 81.

Women were, of course, also affected by the wave of patriotism. Some turned up at recruiting offices, only to be told to 'go home and sit still'. They had to be content with providing 'comforts' for the soldiers. In 1914, Queen Mary appealed for women to support the war effort by knitting hats, gloves and scarves for the soldiers in France and Belgium. They organised the supply of 16 million books and 4 million pairs of socks.

Both the NUWSS and the WSPU suspended their campaigning and the suffragettes actively supported the recruitment drive (see page 95). Hundreds of women took a pledge:

> At this hour of England's peril, I do hereby pledge myself most solemnly in the name of my King and Country to persuade every man I know to offer his services to his country. I also pledge myself never to be seen in public with any man who, being in every way fit and free for service, has refused to respond to his country's call.

Posters like this one encouraged girls to put pressure on their boyfriends.

TO THE YOUNG WOMEN OF LONDON

Is your "Best Boy" wearing Khaki? If not don't **YOU THINK** he should be?

If he does not think that you and your country are worth fighting for—do you think he is **WORTHY** of you?

Don't pity the girl who is alone—her young man is probably a soldier—fighting for her and her country—and for **YOU**.

If your young man neglects his duty to his King and Country, the time may come when he will **NEGLECT YOU**.

Think it over—then ask him to

JOIN THE ARMY TO-DAY

▲ British propaganda poster, 1915

Women and the call for volunteers

The war released women to show their capacity for organisation, hard work, persistence and responsibility, unused in the restricted gender roles of the Victorian and Edwardian period.

Many thousands joined the Voluntary Aid Detachment (VAD). These volunteers, mainly from the middle class, provided nursing services at first in Britain but later behind the lines in France as well. This painting from the time shows these volunteer nurses preparing bandages and other medical equipment.

On Thursday 13 October 1914, as casualties mounted on the Western Front and military hospitals in the UK struggled to cope with the vast numbers of wounded arriving each day, a telegram was dispatched from VAD headquarters to detachment commanders, telling them to prepare for the arrival of a particularly large number of casualties in urgent need of help.

Ninety-six detachments were mobilised and in addition to hospitals, they prepared church and village halls, chapel schoolrooms and empty houses. Just before noon the following day, 3000 wounded British and Belgian soldiers were being safely cared for in beds in hospitals, mobilised and prepared by the Voluntary Aid Detachments.

▼ A painting showing British volunteer nurses at work, c. 1915

Reflect

What impression does this painting give of VAD volunteers?

Women and paid work

Initially, the war meant that many working women lost their jobs as the fashion and fishing industries were disrupted. But conscription changed everything. With many more men now being called up, women from all classes stepped into a wide variety of jobs traditionally done by men; this image shows them working as builder's labourers. Photographers took many pictures of women taking on physically demanding work but the attention given to these photographs can be misleading. Many of the jobs women took were in traditional female roles. As well as nurses, 200,000 women worked in government departments and another 500,000 in office jobs, for example in banks. The number of women in employment increased from 3.2 million in 1914 to 4.8 million in 1918.

▲ Women labourers, 1917

Land Girls

In total 80,000 women joined the Women's Land Army, as 'Land Girls'. They took on all aspects of farming including ploughing the fields with teams of horses. Agnes Greatorex left her job as a maid to become a Land Girl:

> We had to get up at five in the morning for milking, and then we'd have to take it up to the hospital. After that – especially during the winter – we'd have to muck-out the cow sheds. Then we might get half an hour for breakfast. I'd be out there picking up stones from the field or cutting hay, and I'd be as happy as a lark. I had a pound a week, not as much as the men but a lot still – there was no-one to boss me, no more running around at the beck and call of the cook.

Reflect

Farm work was hard, yet Agnes Greatorex, and many like her, preferred it to being a domestic servant. What did she like about it?

Heavy industry

Women were also in demand in heavy industries, like shipbuilding and engineering. They were not always welcomed by the men they worked alongside. Dorothy Poole recalled:

▼ Women operating heavy machinery, 1918

> Over and over again the foreman gave me wrong or incomplete instructions or altered them in such a way as to make me work more hours. None of the men spoke to me for a long time and would give me no help as to where to find things. My drawer was nailed up by the men and oil was poured over everything through a crack one night.

The men were concerned about their own jobs and pay. Women were doing the same job for less pay and the men feared that employers would lower their wages to match. Another problem was 'dilution'. This meant breaking down tasks into smaller components, particularly in engineering, so that the women, newly arrived in the factory and less skilled, could carry them out. Skilled workers were concerned that their more highly paid, skilled jobs could disappear. Their trade unions supported them and there was a series of strikes in May 1917. Under DORA the strikers could have been sent to prison, but the government was determined to work with the trade unions. Eventually a deal was made with the trade unions that dilution would only last as long as the war.

Munitions workers

Lloyd George organised the building of huge new munitions factories that needed large numbers of workers. Posters like the one on page 83 called on women to take these jobs. By 1917, 947,000women were employed in the industry. In 1976 one of them recalled how eagerly women flocked to munitions work:

> I was in domestic service when the war broke out and hated every minute of it, earning £2 a month working from 6.00 a.m. to 9.00 p.m. So when the need came for women 'war-workers' my chance came to 'get out'. I started on hand cutting shell fuses. We worked twelve hours a day, apart from the journey morning and night. As for wages, I thought I was very well off earning £5 a week.

▲ A munitions factory at Chilwell, near Nottingham, 1917

Women were glad to earn their own money and be free of the restrictions of domestic service. But it was dangerous work. There were fatal explosions at some munitions factories and the TNT (a chemical used in the explosives) turned their skins yellow, earning them the nickname of 'canary girls'. Many women became seriously ill from the chemicals they were handling.

On the other hand, employing so many women improved working conditions in many factories. There was the need for separate toilets and decent washrooms. Rest rooms began to be provided, as well as canteens and nurseries for women with small children. Workers were given regular health checks. Improved working conditions and welfare at work were among the lasting benefits of the war.

Most of the women who worked in the war gave up their jobs when the war ended – or were forced to: the number of working women in 1920 was almost the same as in 1914.

This table pulls together the enormous changes in women's employment brought by the war.

Job	Number of women employed	
	1914	1918
Munitions	212,000	947,000
Transport	18,200	117,200
Business	505,200	934,500
Agriculture	190,000	228,000
Government and teaching	262,200	460,200
Hotels and catering	181,000	220,000
Other heavy industry	2,178,600	2,970,600
Domestic service	1,658,000	1,250,000
Nursing and secretarial	542,000	652,500
Self-employed	430,000	470,000

Reflect

1. Find the only job which showed a decline in the number of women employees.
2. Does this surprise you?

Women at home

The war was difficult for women, whether they worked or not. Married women had to endure the painful parting from their husbands, the anxiety of whether he would survive, and the dread of the telegram informing her of his death. Ordinary soldiers' pay was 7s (35p) a week, so they couldn't send much home. Married women were paid a minimal 'separation allowance' of 12s 6d (52.5p) plus 2s (10p) for each child. As you have seen, rationing was introduced late in the war (January 1918). Up until then shortages of essential foods meant long queues and high prices. In particular, 1917 was a year of hunger. Amelia Harris, daughter of a boot repairer in London was ten that year. She recalled:

> Breakfast was tea and bread. At teatime it was bread and dripping. For dinner there was boiled potatoes with cabbage leaves we picked off the floor of the market.

Along with these worries, women had to bring up their families on their own, endure air-raids, and, as the wartime song went: 'Keep the home fires burning'.

Women's suffrage

The women's campaign for the vote was called off as soon as war was declared. Millicent Fawcett promised that the NUWSS organisation would help the war effort. Emmeline Pankhurst, as usual, went further. Having forcefully opposed the government for eight years, she called a halt to all WSPU activity as soon as war was declared and organised a march of 30,000 women calling on the government to let women serve in the war effort. She changed the name of the WSPU newspaper, *The Suffragette* to *Britannia*. She supported the 'White Feather' campaign.

Long before the end of the war, Parliament had to think about how to arrange who was going to vote in the first peacetime election. How could men who had been prepared to die for their country, and women who had served bravely and tirelessly at home, be denied a vote for its government? The suffragists and the suffragettes had already threatened an immediate resumption of their activities if they were to be denied the vote this time.

The old diehards, Asquith in the Commons, Lord Curzon in the Lords, and all their followers, could see that they had to back down. The new suffrage qualification became law in February 1918. All men over 21 except conscientious objectors would have the vote, and all women over 30. This last, ridiculous, proviso was, it seems, because the men in Parliament just could not face an electorate in which women were the majority. So the young women who had filled shells in the munitions factories, milked cows at dawn, driven ambulances in France and all kinds of other jobs, were denied the vote. This final snub was eventually removed in 1928 when women were granted the right to vote on the same basis as men.

▲ An engraving showing a woman casting her vote in the 1918 General Election. Made 1918

Record

Finish the 'response cards' that you have been making based on pages 92–95. They should follow the instructions given on page 81.

Review

1. Look at your full set of 'response cards'.
   - Arrange them in chronological order.
   - Identify key moments of change.
   - Identify responses that were shaped by government propaganda.
   - Identify examples of responses that required self-sacrifice.

2. How far do you agree with the view that the British people can be proud of how they responded to the demands of total war?

Edwardian Britain: 'A golden age'?

▲ A room in Warwick Castle, 2012

History and tourism

This photograph shows two waxwork models set in a room at Warwick Castle in the heart of England. The scene is part of the castle's carefully marketed tourism attraction that invites visitors to experience something of the delights of an Edwardian weekend party in a great country house.

The detail and quality of the Edwardian furnishings and costumes at Warwick Castle perfectly match a popular view of Edwardian England as a golden age of style and contentment that was brutally ended by the arrival of the First World War in 1914. Certainly many British people in the early 1920s saw the pre-war world this way as they struggled with the awful aftermath of the war and the horrors of the Spanish influenza epidemic that followed. The same view was held in the 1930s as the effects of worldwide trade depression threw millions out of work and helped dictators into power in Europe. By 1939 the world was again at war and the attractions of the lost golden age of Edwardian England seemed stronger than ever. They still glow brightly in the tourist world at Warwick Castle. But, as you have learned in this book, we should be doubtful about any version of history that shows Edwardian England as an uncomplicated, settled and orderly society where all was well for one and all.

▲ A London stage-set, 2006

History and theatre

This photograph shows a scene from a theatre production in London's West End in 2006. The play is called *An Inspector Calls* and it was written over 60 years earlier in 1945 by English playwright, J. B. Priestley.

In the remarkable stage setting shown above, the lights are glowing in a large Edwardian house, set apart from any other buildings. Almost all the action in the play happens inside the house in a warm, comfortable dining room.

In his original script, Priestley gives directions that, when the play starts, the people on stage 'have all had a good dinner, are celebrating a special occasion, and are pleased with themselves'. They are all from the wealthy English merchant class, the sort of people for whom the Edwardian era was a golden age. As if to help the audience appreciate their comfort, Priestley says that the lighting in the room should be 'pink and intimate' – what we might call a rose-tinted glow.

All that changes when another character, an 'inspector' (shown above), appears out of the mists, knocks on the door and is shown into the dining room. At that point, says Priestley, the lighting should become 'brighter and harder'. For the rest of the play, the inspector gradually uncovers layers of life and connections between the characters and reveals all sorts of underlying hypocrisy. By the end of the play, far from being 'pleased with themselves', they are deeply divided and disturbed.

Priestley wrote the play immediately after the Second World War at a time when some people still argued that Britain needed to get back to the world as it was before 1914. He wanted to show his audience that the new society that they had to build after the Second World War had to make much more radical changes. He used the lives of the characters in his play to argue that Edwardian Britain was no 'Golden Age'. It was deeply unhealthy and should not serve as a model for the future. Priestley was using drama to interpret history.

Why history matters

Priestley's play asks timeless questions about what values a society should be based on as it tries to build a better future. Such questions can only be answered by a close and probing inspection of the past followed by open debate.

Interpretations of history matter.

Preparing for the examination

The British depth study forms the second half of Paper 1: British History. It is worth 20 per cent of your GCSE. To succeed in the examination you will need to think clearly about different aspects of Britain in Peace and War, 1900–1918, and to support your ideas with accurate knowledge. This section suggests some revision strategies and explains the types of examination questions that you can expect.

 ## Summaries of the five key issues

Your study of Britain in Peace and War, 1900–18, has covered five important issues from that time:

1. Wealth: tensions in Edwardian society
2. Politics: threats to political stability
3. Women: the nature and extent of support for women's suffrage
4. Empire: British attitudes towards the Empire
5. War: responses to the demands of total war.

In the specification for your GCSE course, each of the five issues is divided into three sections. We divided each enquiry in this book into three stages to match these sections and to help you build your knowledge and understanding step by step.

Now you can use your knowledge and understanding to produce a detailed and accurate summary for each of the five issues. You will also need to be clear about how the five issues are connected. Here are four suggestions for structuring your revision notes and showing the connections between the issues. Choose the one that is best for you or use a variety if you prefer.

I. Mind maps

A mind map on A3 paper (or even larger) is a good way to summarise the important points about a particular issue. It allows you to show connections between different points. This is especially important in the British depth study as you are expected to show the interplay between issues (how one issue may affect others).

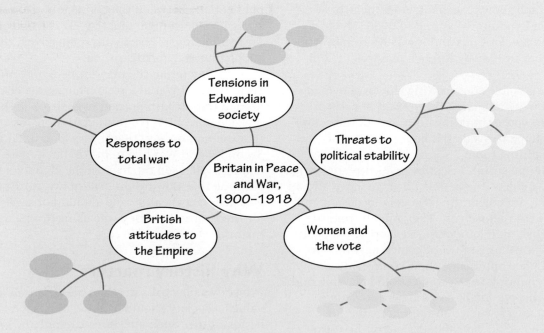

2. Charts

If you find it easier to learn from lists then a summary chart for each of the five issues you have studied might be best for you. You can use the format shown on the right or design your own. Just make sure that you include clear summary points for each of the three sections in each enquiry you studied.

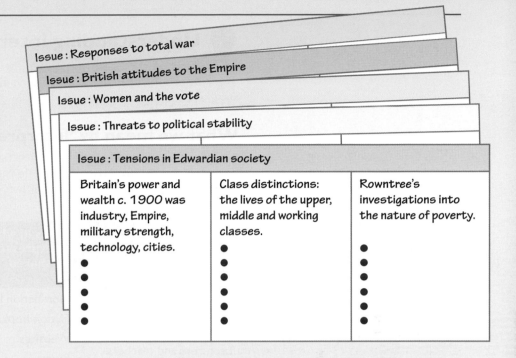

Issue : Responses to total war

Issue : British attitudes to the Empire

Issue : Women and the vote

Issue : Threats to political stability

Issue : Tensions in Edwardian society

Britain's power and wealth c. 1900 was industry, Empire, military strength, technology, cities.	Class distinctions: the lives of the upper, middle and working classes.	Rowntree's investigations into the nature of poverty.
●	●	●
●	●	●
●	●	●
●	●	●
●	●	●

3. Small cards

Small cards are a flexible way to make revision notes. You could create a set of revision cards for each of the five main issues/enquiries you have studied. It would be a good idea to use a different colour for each set of cards.

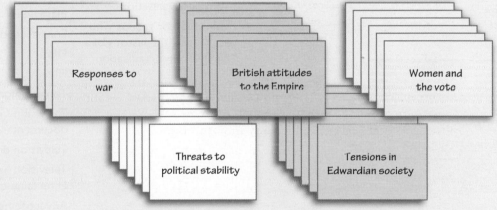

Responses to war

British attitudes to the Empire

Women and the vote

Threats to political stability

Tensions in Edwardian society

4. Podcasts

If you learn best by listening to information and explanations, you could record your knowledge and understanding by producing podcasts to summarise what you have learned about each of the five main issues. You could produce your podcast with a friend, using a question and answer format.

To be well prepared for the examination you need revision notes that summarise the main points and provide detailed examples in a format that works best for you.

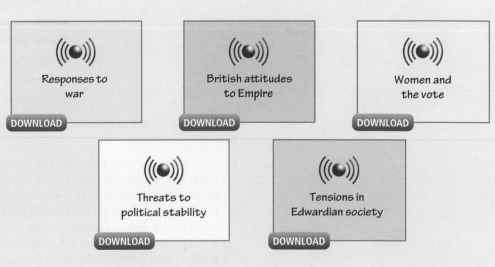

Responses to war
DOWNLOAD

British attitudes to Empire
DOWNLOAD

Women and the vote
DOWNLOAD

Threats to political stability
DOWNLOAD

Tensions in Edwardian society
DOWNLOAD

Understanding interpretations

To prepare for the examination, you will need to be clear about 'interpretations of history'. Here are some simple explanations and some suggestions for your revision.

What we mean by 'interpretations' of history

An interpretation of history is any version of events in the past that has been created at some later time. The interpretation can be made and shared by all sorts of people in all sorts of ways for all sorts of reasons. Here are some examples:

People or groups who create or advise on interpretations of the past	Ways in which interpretations may be shared	Reasons for creating interpretations of the past
Academics (professional historians, museum curators or archaeologists)	Non-fiction books	To educate or inform
	Fiction books	To entertain or amuse
Lecturers and teachers	Websites	To persuade
Writers and artists	Blogs	To commemorate
Tourist organisations	Exhibitions and displays	
Individuals or groups who are tracing the history of a family or an organisation	Magazines	
	Formal reports and articles	
	Plays	
	Films	
	Tourist information boards	
	Television / radio documentaries	
	Television dramas	
	Television light entertainment	
	Advertisements	
	Background to news reports	
	Drawings and paintings	
	Computer games	
	Theme parks	
	Souvenirs	
	Monuments	
	Ceremonies	

These tasks will help to sharpen your thinking about historical interpretations:

1. **Try to match up each of the people or groups in the left column with the methods you think they might use to share their interpretations and the reasons why they have created them.**
2. **Look back through this book to find examples of historical interpretations. For each one you find ...**
   - **briefly summarise what historical point it makes**
   - **list who created it, how it was shared with other people and what its purpose was.**

How interpretations of the past may differ

People who look back on the past often disagree about what they find. They may disagree about all sorts of issues including:

- what actually happened and when
- whether an event or type of behaviour was 'typical' of the period in history when it happened
- why events or developments happened at all or why they happened at a certain time
- which person, factor or consequence was most significant and why
- how much change was happening, how quickly and how it affected different groups of people at the time
- what sources should be used and what they reveal
- what (if anything) we can learn from the events of the past.

Why interpretations of the past may differ

There are many different reasons why people offer different interpretations of the past. Here are a few suggestions:

- They may use different sources, for example, someone working at a later date may be able to use newly discovered documents or new scientific techniques to throw more light on the issue.
- They may be faced with gaps in the evidence and may make different but reasonable guesses based on the sources they have.
- They use the same sources very carefully but honestly reach different conclusions.
- They are affected by their own background or context; for example, the age in which they were working, their nationality, personality, beliefs and values may all affect their judgements.
- They may be creating their interpretation for different groups of people, for example, young children or foreign tourists rather than professional historians.
- They may be creating their interpretations for different reasons, for example, to provide light-hearted entertainment rather than precise historical understanding.
- They may simply be less careful in applying good historical methods, for example, failing to consider all available sources, misunderstanding what sources say, reaching conclusions that cannot be supported by the sources or failing to make their conclusions clear.

This depth study forms the second half of Paper 1: British History. It is worth 20 per cent of your GCSE. The whole exam lasts for 1 hour and 45 minutes so you will have just over 50 minutes to answer the three questions on Britain in Peace and War, 1900–1918.

Question 6a

You will be shown an interpretation of some aspect of your course on Britain in Peace and War, 1900–1918. It may be in text form or an image. The question will start by telling you the point that the interpretation is making. You will have to show that you understand how it does this. The question will usually begin *'In Interpretation A the historian … Identify and explain one way in which the historian does this'*.

Example

6 (a) In Interpretation A the artist Richard Hook tries to portray some of the drama of life in Britain in the early twentieth century. Identify one way in which the artist does this.   (3 marks)

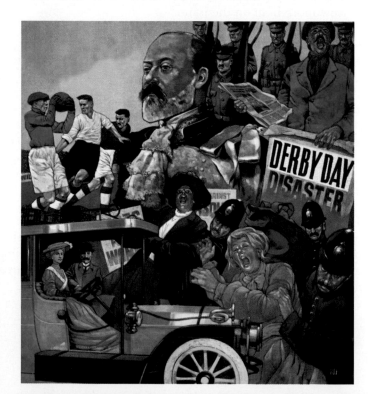

Devise five questions like this using different interpretations that you can find in this book. Try to use images with one or two and text with the others.

Question 6b

Question 6b

You will be asked to suggest an area of further research into an aspect of the historical situation or issue that is the focus of question 6a. You will have to justify the suggestion you make. The stem will usually be *'If you were asked to do further research on [Interpretation A], what would you choose to investigate? Explain how this would help us to analyse and understand [the topic in 6a].*

> **6** (b) If you were asked to do further research on one aspect of Interpretation A, what would you choose to investigate? Explain how this would help us to analyse and understand life in Britain in the early twentieth century. (5 marks)

For each of the questions you invented for 6a (see page 102), write a brief 6b style question.

Question 7

Question 7 requires you to explain how far and why two given interpretations differ. A typical stem is 'Interpretations B and C both focus on …. How far do they differ and what might explain any differences?'

Example

7 Interpretations B and C both focus on the force-feeding of suffragettes. How far do they differ and what might explain the difference? **(12 marks)**

Interpretation B – An extract from *Dying for the Vote*, a secondary school textbook written by Jane Richardson and Ian Dawson in 2002

The woman was held down and a tube was pushed up her nose. A milky liquid was poured into a funnel connected to the rubber tube. This was extremely painful. The government ordered force-feeding to stop hunger strikers dying as this would cause a lot of bad publicity. In 1913 the government brought in a new law, known as the 'Cat and Mouse Act'. This allowed hunger strikers to be released until their health improved and then they would be re-arrested to complete their sentences.

Interpretation C – An extract from *The Making of Modern Britain*, a history book written for the general public by the journalist Andrew Marr in 2009

The force-feeding of women in prison who had gone on hunger strike was itself a brutal business. Trying to force mouths open to accommodate metal contraptions resulted in broken teeth and ripped gums; alternatively, the passages of the nose would be bruised by rubber tubes shoved down into the stomach. In Holloway prison in London, a twenty-one-year-old working-class girl from Leicester who had trained as a dancer, Lillian Lenton, was subjected to force-feeding and had the tube accidentally pushed into her windpipe. Her left lung was filled with sloppy food and she nearly died […] Hurriedly released, her case led to the 'Cat and Mouse Act' which provided for very ill suffragettes to be released from prison, watched until they recovered, and then arrested and jailed again.

Practise this type of question by using the example above. Find differences in:

- **What the two interpretations say**
- **What one interpretations includes that the other does not**
- **How the two interpretations are written, i.e. their style and tone.**

Then try to explain why these differences might exist. You could use the list on page 101 to get you started but you should only use an idea from that list if you can back up your suggestion with good reasons to show that it might apply in this particular case.

Question 8/9

You have a choice of two judgement questions: Question 8 or Question 9. These questions in the second part of Paper 1 are the most challenging. They ask you make a judgement about a particular interpretation of an aspect of life in Britain 1900–1918. You need to save enough time for this question because it is worth 20 marks.

Example

8 In an article in the *Daily Mail* newspaper in 2015 the historian A.N. Wilson stated that, in the period before the First World War, 'life for the majority of men and women was hellish'. How far do you agree with this view? (20 marks)

9 By calling his 1995 book *The Age of Upheaval: Edwardian Politics 1899–1914*, the historian David Brooks suggests that there were big changes in British politics during that period. How far do you agree with this view? (20 marks)

Depending on the interpretation given in the question, you may wish to agree completely or disagree completely or take a position where you can see some reasons for agreeing and some for disagreeing. You can get full marks for any of these types of answer provided that you:

- show that you have understood exactly what the interpretation is claiming
- show that you understand any particularly important words, phrases or dates that the interpretation uses
- use very clear explanations and suitable accurate supporting evidence to persuade the examiner that you are giving a very reasonable answer
- keep closely to the point all the way through your answer.

In the examples above, are there any words, phrases or dates in the interpretations that you would need to address in your answer?

Choose one of the example questions above and write a plan of how you would answer it. It is helpful to plan each paragraph in your answer so that it has a very definite main point that is clearly supported with accurate and appropriate evidence chosen from your knowledge of the period.

Glossary

act the name given in Parliament to something that creates a new law. (See also 'Bill')

apathy lack of interest

aristocrat a member of the ruling elite

Baptists Christians who believe that believers should be baptised as adults. They are not part of the Church of England and tend to have support from the middle and working classes

bill the name given in Parliament to something that is being discussed as a possible new law. (See also 'Act')

Boer War a war fought in South Africa between Britain and white South African farmers known as Boers (1899–1902)

borstals schools that held and tried to reform young offenders

cabinet the group of senior politicians who control government policy

cable telegraph a system for sending messages usually in Morse code along wires bound together in a waterproof sleeve

capitalism a system of running a nation where wealth is created and controlled by individuals for their own profit, rather than by the state.

censorship government control of information

census a government record of the population made every ten years

chancellor of the exchequer the member of the government directly responsible for the nation's wealth, setting the level of national taxation

colony an area of land controlled and inhabited by people from another country

concentration camp a place where the enemies of a country are imprisoned. First use by the British during the Boer War

Congregationalists Christians who believe that each church group should govern its own affairs. They are not part of the Church of England and tend to have support from the middle and working classes

conscription forcing people to join the armed services

debutante a wealthy young woman making her first official appearance at a fashionable event

diplomat an official who represents his country in discussions with other nations

domestic service the employment of servants to do jobs on the house

Durbar a royal, public celebration in India

electorate the total group of people who vote in an election

empire lands ruled by one country

Fabian Society a British socialist organisation

Fenians (Irish Republican Brotherhood) an Irish group that wanted Ireland to be a separate, self-governing nation

friendly societies associations originally set up by groups of working people to save money and create a fund for to help those in immediate need e.g. through illness or unemployment

House of Commons the part of the British Parliament where MPs (Members of Parliament) elected by people in different areas help to make laws and to debate national issues

House of Lords the part of the British Parliament where Lords (people with titles such as a duke or a bishop) help to make laws and debate national issues

hung parliament a House of Commons where no single party has enough MPs to outvote the rest

hunger strike the refusal to eat used as a form of protest

insanitary lacking clean water and toilets

Irish Home Rule a policy that would allow the people of Ireland to have their own Parliament while remaining part of the United Kingdom

labour exchanges places where unemployed people tried to help getting a job

lords (peers) high-ranking people with titles such as a duke or a bishop

martial law the name given to any situation where ordinary laws are suspended for a time while the army takes charge

martyr a person who dies for a cause they believe in

Methodists Christians who follow the relatively simple style of worship encouraged by John Wesley. They are not part of the Church of England and tend to have support from the middle and working classes

militant extreme e.g. a person who is willing to use violence to advance their cause

moderate not extreme

munitions weapons and ammunition

patriotism pride in your country

poor law guardians members of the community who ran the workhouse where local poor, unemployed and often elderly people lived

poverty line the point where a person or family are officially seen as 'poor' by society

propaganda widely spread, one-sided information used to promote a particular point of view